UNBEARABLY GOOD!
MOCHI LOVERS COOKBOOK

Compiled by

Teresa DeVirgilio-Lam
5239 Kalanianaole Hwy.
Honolulu, HI 96821

This cookbook is a product of
*Cookbooks by Morris Press **Type 'N $ave**™ program.*
All recipes were typed by the customer.

Printed in the U.S.A. by
Cookbooks by Morris Press
P.O. Box 2110 • Kearney, NE 68848

For information on having your
cookbook printed, write for our FREE information
packet or call Toll-Free at 1-800-445-6621.

DEDICATION

This book is dedicated to my family, friends and fellow mochi lovers:

To my husband, Gregory Lam, for his love, support and encouragement. May you always walk beside me and share in my achievements in life.

To my parents, Louis and Sadie DeVirgilio, they have always believed in me. They have encouraged me to follow my dreams and have always loved me in my successes and failures.

To my 2 year old triplets, Ashlyn, Gabrielle and Alexis, they are the greatest joy and love of all our lives.

To my husband's parents Ruth and Wallace Lam, for all of their support and help with my children and new adventures.

Special thanks to Michelle and Danny Abreu, Margaret Gallegos, Wendy and Randall Nagano, Leilyn Kojima and Phyllis Uyeda for their support and encouragement with my first cookbook, "Unbearably Good! Mochi and Mochi Rice Desserts." Most of all, a big mahalo for their friendship!

TERESA A. DEVIRGILIO-LAM WITH DAUGHTERS GABRIELLE, ASHLYN AND ALEXIS

Teresa DeVirgilio-Lam was born the fourth out of six children to Sadie Rika Yoshida and Louis Francis DeVirgilio. Her parents decided to raise their brood of children in Kailua. From an early age, Teresa enjoyed baking and cooking goodies for her family. This joy of cooking led Teresa into the wonderful world of "Food and Beverage."

Teresa is a graduate from the University of Hawaii, Food Science and Human Nutrition Program and from Kapiolani Community College, Food and Beverage Program.

For the past 15 years, Teresa has managed restaurants and other food and beverage departments in Hawaii hotels. She worked as a Room Service Manager at the former Kahala Hilton. There she personally worked with and served President and Mrs. Clinton, the Emperor and Empress of Japan, the Sultan of Brunei and many other dignitaries and stars.

Previously, Teresa was a manager at the Hawaiian Regent Hotel, Sheraton Princess Kaiulani Hotel and the Sheraton Princeville Hotel. Presently, she is a manager at TGI Friday's in Honolulu and a full time mother of triplets. Even though Teresa is very busy, she finds time to cook her favorite mochi desserts for her family and friends.

GLOSSARY

Mochi — glutinous rice cake
Mochiko — glutinous rice flour
Mochi gome — uncooked glutinous rice

An — red bean paste
Azuki Beans — Beans that vary in color from dark red to cream, beans are available dried or in cans.
Goma — sesame seeds
Hung jo — Chinese dried red dates
Imo — sweet potato
Karabasa — pumpkin
Kinako — soy bean flour
Koshi — mashed bean paste
Nantu — steamed Okinawan mochi
Nantuisu — Okinawan New Year's pudding
Palm sugar — A strong flavored dark sugar from the sap of coconut palms and Palmyrah palms. Substitute dark brown sugar if unavailable.
Rose water — If you can't buy, soak cleaned rose petals overnight in water. Remove petals and use water in recipe.
Taimo — taro
Tsubushi an — mashed azuki beans
Wong tong — Chinese brown sugar
Yamaimo — mountain yam

Mochi

AGE MOCHI

1 box mochiko
1½ c. water
1 tsp. sugar
pinch of salt

Mix together the mochiko, water, sugar and salt in a large mixing bowl. Beat the mixture until it is smooth. Pour batter into a microwavable bundt pan. Cover pan with Saran wrap. Microwave on medium for three minutes. Rotate pan and microwave on high for an additional three minutes. Scoop mochi out and form into 2 inch oval shapes while still warm. Roll oval in furikake. Deep fry ovals until brown and crispy. Serve in saimin or with nori sauce!

AN MOCHI

2⅔ c. water
1 c. white sugar
3 c. mochiko
½ tsp. salt
1 c. cornstarch
1 can koshi or tsubushian
potato starch or cornstarch to dust

Combine water and sugar in sauce pan and bring to a boil. Boil for several minutes. In a large mixing bowl, combine mochiko and salt. Make a well in center of flour mixture and add hot sugar syrup. Mix until ingredients are well blended. Knead dough on a board sprinkled with cornstarch for 3 to 5 minutes. Dough should be smooth and elastic. Pinch off walnut size pieces of dough and flatten to form circles. Fill center of each circle with a tablespoon of bean paste. Fold up dough and pinch ends together to form a ball. Dust with potato or corn starch.

AN MOCHI 2

2²/₃ c. water
1 c. white sugar
3 c. mochiko
½ tsp. salt
1 c. cornstarch
1 can koshi or tsubushian
potato starch or cornstarch to dust

Combine water and sugar in sauce pan and bring to a boil. Boil for several minutes. In a large mixing bowl, combine mochiko and salt. Make a well in center of flour mixture and add hot sugar syrup. Mix until ingredients are well blended. Knead dough on a board sprinkled with cornstarch for 3 to 5 minutes. Dough should be smooth and elastic. Pinch off walnut size pieces of dough and flatten to form circles. Fill center of each circle with a tablespoon of bean paste. Fold up dough and pinch ends together to form a ball. Dust with potato or corn starch.

APRICOT JELLO MOCHI

1 box mochiko
2 boxes apricot Jello
1½ c. white sugar
1 can apricot nectar - 12 oz.
12 oz. water
potato starch or cornstarch - to dust at the end of cooking

Preheat oven to 350°. Mix Jello, sugar, and mochiko together in a large bowl. Add juice and water to flour mixture and mix well. Pour into a greased and floured 9 x 13-inch pan. Cover entire pan with a piece of foil and bake for one hour. Remove pan from oven and cool. Cut mochi after it has cooled completely. Roll in potato starch or cornstarch.

Cindy Gieger

27324-99

Azuki meshi

³/₄ c. mochi gome
³/₄ c. azuki beans
³/₄ tsp. salt
1 T. sake - rice wine
2 T. toasted sesame seeds

Wash rice several times. Soak the rice in 2 c. of boiling water for 2 hours. Meanwhile, clean the beans and place them in a heavy stock pot with 4 c. of water. Bring to boil, then lower heat and simmer gentle for 30 minutes. Add ½ tsp. salt and continue to simmer for an additional 30 minutes. Drain the beans and save the liquid. Drain the rice and place in a saucepan with ¼ tsp. salt, 1 c. plus 2 T. bean liquid and the beans. Bring to boil. Cover and lower heat to **low** and simmer for 20 minutes. Add sake to the rice mixture and cook an additional 5 minutes. Sprinkle sesame seeds over top and serve warm.

Azuki nantu

4 c. mochiko
1³/₄ c. white sugar
½ tsp. salt
3 c. water
1 c. azuki beans
kinako for dusting

Wash azuki beans. Cover with water and bring to a boil. Lower heat and simmer for 45 minutes. Drain azuki beans and save liquid. Add water to bean water to make 3 cups. Pour into mixing bowl. Add mochiko and salt, mix well. Pour into double thickness cheese cloth and steam for 45 minutes. Immediately place mochi into a mixing bowl and stir in the sugar. Add food coloring if desired and azuki beans to mochi and mix well. Pour mochi into a 9 x 9 inch pan that has been dusted with kinako. Cool for at least 6 hours before cutting.

BADUYA KARABASA

20 oz. mochiko
3/4 c. brown sugar
1 c. cooked and mashed pumpkin - karabasa
1 can coconut milk
Oil for deep frying

Mix mochiko, sugar, pumpkin and coconut milk together until a soft dough is formed. Heat oil. Drop by tablespoonful into hot oil. Cook until golden brown. Balls should float to top of oil when done.

BAKED BIBINGKA

5 c. mochiko
3 c. packed dark brown sugar
1 T. baking soda
1 can coconut milk
2 1/2 c. water
2 T. sesame seeds

Preheat oven to 350°. Grease and line a 9 x 13-inch pan with wilted banana leaves. Place mochiko, brown sugar and baking soda in a large mixing bowl. Slowly add water and coconut milk to dry ingredients. Stir until mixture is smooth. Pour batter into the prepared pan. Sprinkle with sesame seeds. Bake for 1 hour. Cool for several hours. Cut with plastic knife.

27324-99

BAKED CAKE MOCHI

2 c. mochiko
2 c. brown sugar
1 T. baking soda
2 beaten eggs
12 oz. evaporated milk
12 oz. coconut milk
1/4 c. melted butter or margarine
1 tsp. vanilla
Sesame seeds - optional

Preheat oven to 325°. Grease a 9 x 13-inch baking pan. Sift mochiko, sugar and baking soda into a large mixing bowl. Add coconut milk, evaporated milk, butter, eggs and vanilla to dry ingredients and mix well. Pour into prepared pan and sprinkle with sesame seeds. Bake for 1 hour. Let cake mochi stand for at least 6 hours before cutting with a plastic knife.

BAKED CHI CHI DANGO

1 lb. box mochiko
2 1/2 c. white sugar
1 can coconut milk
2 c. water
red food coloring
potato starch for dusting

Preheat oven to 350°. Grease a 9 x 13-inch pan. Mix the mochiko and sugar together in a large bowl. Add coconut milk, water and several drops of food coloring to flour mixture. Mix until batter is smooth. Pour into prepared pan. Cover pan tightly with foil. Bake for 1 hour. Remove from oven and cool for 5 minutes. Carefully remove foil and let mochi cool for at least 2 hours before cutting. Dust pieces with potato starch to prevent sticking.

Baked Coconut Mochi with Azuki Beans

20 oz. mochiko
2 c. brown sugar
1 T. baking soda
½ tsp. salt
1 can koshian or tsubushian
2 cans coconut milk
1 can water
kinako or potato starch to dust

Preheat oven to 350°. Grease a 9 x 13-inch pan. Sift mochiko, sugar, baking soda and salt together into a large mixing bowl. Add coconut milk, water and koshian to flour mixture. Mix well. Pour batter into prepared pan. Bake for 1 hour. Remove from oven and cool. Cut with a plastic knife and roll piece in kinako or potato starch.

Baked Coconut Nantu

2 pkgs. mochiko - 10 oz. each
1 lb. box light brown sugar
1 T. baking soda
1 can coconut milk
2½ cups water
shredded coconut or sesame seeds to garnish.

Preheat oven to 350°. Grease a 9 x 13-inch pan. Mix mochiko, sugar and baking soda in a large mixing bowl. Add coconut milk and water. Stir until batter is smooth. Pour batter into pan and sprinkle top of batter with shredded coconut and sesame seeds. Bake for 1 hour. Cool mochi completely before cutting.

27324-99

BAKED FILIPINO MOCHI

5 c. mochiko
1½ c. coconut milk
3 c. white sugar
1 small can condensed cream

Preheat oven to 300°. Grease and foil line a 9 x 13-inch pan. Mix the mochiko and sugar in a large mixing bowl. Measure coconut milk and ¾ can of cream with enough water to make liquids equal 3½ cups. Add liquid to flour mixture and mix until smooth. Pour into prepared pan. Bake for ½ hour. Brush top with reserved ¼ can cream. Bake for an additional 1 hour. Cool and slice.

BAKED GAU WITH YAMS

2 pkgs. of mochiko - 10 oz. each
1 lb. brown sugar
⅓ c. shredded coconut
2 T. oil
1 lb. can yams
½ c. liquid from yams
½ c. water
2 tsp. sesame seeds
1 piece dried red date - hung jo

Preheat oven to 375°. Grease a round casserole pan and line with ti leaves. In a large mixing bowl mash the yams. Add the sugar and coconut and blend. Add oil, water and the liquid from the yams and blend. Add the mochiko. Mix until the batter is smooth. Pour batter into prepared pan with ti leaves. Sprinkle sesame seeds on top of batter. Place date in middle of gau. Wrap pan tightly with aluminum foil. Bake for 2 hours. Cool several hours before cutting. Preferably over night.

BAKED MOCHI

5 c. mochiko
3 c. brown sugar
1 tsp. baking soda
1 can coconut milk
2 c. water
1 tsp. vanilla
2 T. sesame seeds

Preheat oven to 350°. Mix mochiko, sugar, baking soda, milk, vanilla and water in large mixing bowl. Stir batter until it is smooth. Pour into a greased and floured 10 x 15½-inch pan. Sprinkle sesame seeds on top of mochi. Bake for forty-five minutes. Remove pan from oven and cool.

BANANA PUDDING MOCHI

2 c. mochiko
1 c. white sugar
4 T. instant banana pudding
2 c. water
2 tsp. vanilla
½ potato starch or kinako

Grease a 8-inch glass or microwave pan. Stir the mochiko, sugar and pudding together in a medium size mixing bowl. Add the vanilla and 1¾ c. water to the mixture. Beat until smooth. Add the additional ¼ c. water if mochi is to thick. Consistency should be like a cake mix. Cover mochi with plastic wrap securely. Microwave mochi for 2 minutes on high power. Rotate pan. Microwave an additional 3 minutes until mochi has set. Remove from microwave and take off the plastic wrap. Let mochi cool for at least ½ hour. Dust a surface with potato starch or kinako. Pour mochi onto the dusted surface and cut into ½ inch squares with a plastic knife. Coat pieces completely with the starch or kinako.

27324-99

BIBINGKA

4 c. mochiko
2 c. white sugar
1 can evaporated milk
1 c. butter or margarine
4 eggs
1 can coconut milk

Preheat oven to 375°. Mix mochiko and sugar together. Add evaporated milk, eggs, coconut milk and melted butter. Stir until smooth. Pour batter into greased and floured 9 x 13-inch pan. Bake one hour. Remove pan from oven and cool.

BIBINGKA ROYALE

2 c. mochiko
4 tsp. baking powder
³/₄ c. white sugar
¹/₂ c. grated cheddar cheese
3 eggs
1¹/₄ c. coconut milk
¹/₂ c. melted butter or margarine
1 c. shredded coconut
2 T. white sugar

Preheat oven to 350°. Grease a 9 x 13-inch pan and line with wilted banana or ti leaves. Combine ³/₄ c. white sugar with coconut milk. Set aside. Beat eggs until light in color. Sift mochiko and baking powder into a large mixing bowl. Gradually add coconut milk mixture. Beat until smooth. Add eggs and ¹/₄ c. melted butter and mix until batter is smooth. Pour batter into prepared pan. Bake for 35-45 minutes or until mochi is set. Remove from oven and promptly brush top with ¹/₄ c. melted butter. Sprinkle the cheese and ¹/₄ c. sugar over melted butter. Sprinkle shredded coconut over the cheese. Cool completely before cutting.

BIBINGKA ROYALE 2

2 c. mochiko
3/4 c. brown sugar
4 tsp. baking powder
1 1/4 c. coconut milk
1/4 c. melted butter
2 c. shredded coconut
1 tsp. vanilla
3 eggs, beaten until light

Preheat oven to 350°. Mix sugar, coconut milk and vanilla together in a large mixing bowl. Sift mochiko and baking powder together. Add mochiko mixture to milk mixture. Beat until dough is smooth. Add eggs and melted butter to batter. Beat mixture until smooth. Pour batter into a greased 9 x 13-inch pan that has been lined with wilted banana leaves. Bake for 45 minutes. Remove from oven and sprinkle with shredded coconut while still hot. Cool completely before cutting.

BIKO

2 1/2 lb. mochi rice
1 can coconut milk
1/2 lb. light brown sugar
1/2 lb. dark brown sugar
1 tsp. vanilla
1 can jack fruit - drained
ti or banana leaves

Rinse rice. Place rice and 6 c. water into a rice cooker and cook like normal. Preheat oven to 350°. Grease a 9 x 13-inch pan and line with wilted banana or ti leaves. Mix coconut milk and dark brown sugar together and set aside. Stir light brown sugar, vanilla, chopped jack fruit and 1/2 c. coconut mixture into hot rice. mix well. Pour rice mixture into prepared pan. Level rice mixture in pan. Pour remaining coconut mixture on top of rice. Bake for 20 minutes. Cool. Cut into squares.

27324-99

BUNUELOS

2 c. mochiko
1/4 c. white sugar
1 tsp. baking powder
1 c. shredded coconut
1 c. water
oil for deep frying
1/2 c. white sugar

Mix mochiko, 1/4 c. white sugar, baking powder and coconut together in a mixing bowl. Add water and mix until smooth. Dough should not be to wet or dry. Shape dough into walnut size balls and fry for 10 minutes or golden brown. Remove from oil and drain on paper towels. Roll mochi balls in sugar while still warm.

BUTSE

17 oz. can of yams
1 lb. box mochiko
18 oz. can sweetened azuki beans
1 quart oil for deep frying

Pour yams and liquid into a large mixing bowl and mash. Add mochiko to the yams and knead into a dough. Roll dough into balls the size of walnuts. Press a hole in the center of the ball and fill with 1 tsp. of the azuki beans. Cover the hole with more dough and reshape into a ball. Place balls on a piece of wax paper while heating the oil to 375°. Deep fry until golden brown, drain.

BUTTER MOCHI

½ c. melted butter
3 c. white sugar
2 c. evaporated milk
½ c. water
1 lb. box mochiko
3 tsp. baking powder
12 oz. can coconut milk
2 tsp. vanilla

Preheat oven to 350°. Grease and flour a 9 x 13-inch pan. In a large mixing bowl, cream the butter and sugar together. Stir in the evaporated milk and water. Stir in the mochiko and baking powder. Add coconut milk and vanilla. Mix until batter is smooth. Pour into prepared pan. Bake for 1 hour or until toothpick comes out clean. Remove from oven and cool.

Margaret Gallegos

BUTTER MOCHI 2

1 lb. box mochiko
3 c. white sugar
2 tsp. baking powder
2 c. milk
½ c. melted butter
5 beaten eggs
2 tsp. vanilla
12 oz. can coconut milk
1 c. shredded coconut

Preheat oven to 350°. Grease and flour a 9 x 13-inch pan. Sift mochiko, white sugar and baking powder. Add milk, butter, vanilla, eggs and coconut milk to mixture. Mix until batter is smooth. Pour into prepared pan. Bake 1 hour. Top crust should be golden brown. Remove from oven and cool.

Michelle Abreu

27324-99

BUTTER MOCHI 3

1/2 c. butter
1 lb. mochiko
2 1/2 c. white sugar
1 tsp. baking powder
3 c. milk
5 eggs, beaten
1 tsp. vanilla
1 c. shredded coconut

Preheat oven to 350°. Grease a 9 x 13-inch pan. Melt butter and cool. Combine mochiko, sugar and baking powder in a large mixing bowl. Add milk, eggs, vanilla, butter, and shredded coconut to flour mixture and mix well. Pour batter into prepared pan. Bake 1 hour. Cool.

Mary Lou Nash

BUTTER TARO MOCHI

1 lb. box mochiko
1 1/2 c. white sugar
1 c. brown sugar
1/2 c. melted butter
1 tsp. baking powder
3 c. coconut milk
5 eggs, beaten
1 tsp. vanilla
2 c. cooked and grated taro

Preheat oven to 350°. Grease a 9 x 13-inch pan. Melt butter and put aside to cool. Combine mochiko, sugars and baking powder in a large mixing bowl. Add melted butter, coconut milk, eggs and vanilla. Mix until smooth. Stir in taro and mix well. Pour batter into prepared pan. Bake for 1 hour. Remove pan from oven and cool before cutting.

CASCARON

1 lb. box mochiko
3/4 c. packed brown sugar
1 c. coconut milk
2 c. shredded coconut
1 quart oil for frying

Preheat oil to 350° in a deep fryer. Mix mochiko, sugar, coconut and coconut milk together in a large mixing bowl. Mix until a dough forms, but do not over mix. Roll dough into 1 inch balls. Deep fry balls until golden brown, approximately 3 to 4 minutes. Drain on paper towels.

CASCARON 2

2 c. mochiko
1¼ c. coconut milk
½ c. sweetened shredded coconut
1 c. white sugar
¼ c. water
oil for deep frying

Heat deep fryer to 350°. Mix mochiko, coconut milk and coconut in a large mixing bowl. Shape into walnut size balls. If dough is to crumbly add a little more coconut milk. Fry cascaron until golden brown. In a sauce pan, combine sugar and water. Cook till sugar is completely dissolved. Approximately 5 minutes. Place balls in syrup and stir lightly until each ball is well coated with sugar.

27324-99

CASCARON 3

10 oz. mochiko
1/2 c. white sugar
1 tsp. baking powder
1/2 tsp. salt
1 c. shredded coconut
1 c. evaporated milk
2 c. sugar
3/4 c. water
oil for deep frying

Heat oil to 300°. Mix mochiko, 1/2 c. sugar, baking powder, salt and shredded coconut in large mixing bowl. Stir in milk. Dough will be very soft. Drop by heaping teaspoon into hot oil and fry until golden brown. Drain on paper towels. In a sauce pan, combine 2 c. sugar and 3/4 c. water and simmer until light caramel in color. Place cascaron balls in a bowl and pour syrup over and toss quickly. Remove to another plate to cool.

CHI CHI DANGO

2 c. mochiko
1/2 tsp. salt
1 c. milk
4 T. melted butter or margarine
4 T. white sugar

Bring water to a simmer in a large steamer pot. Mix mochiko, sugar and salt together. Add milk and butter. Stir until a soft dough forms. Knead for 30 seconds. Use additional mochiko to prevent sticking. Place several layers of dampened cheese cloth onto steamer tray. Spread dough onto cheese cloth. Dough should be approximately 1/2 inch thick. Cover dough with cheese cloth. Place steamer tray into pot with about an inch of simmering water. Cover pot and steam dough for 20 minutes. Then remove tray and lift cloth containing dough. Remove cloth and place dough on a surface dusted with potato starch. Cool 10 minutes. Knead dough until smooth. Dough should be as hot as you can tolerate when handling. Place mochi in a greased and dusted 9 x 13-inch pan. Smooth. Cool.

Mary Lou Nash

CHI CHI DANGO II

1 lb. box mochiko
2½ c. white sugar
1 tsp. baking powder
1 can coconut milk
1¾ c. water
1 tsp. vanilla

Preheat oven to 350°. Grease a 9 x 13-inch pan. Mix together the mochiko, sugar and baking powder in a large mixing bowl. Add the coconut milk, water and vanilla and mix until batter is smooth. Pour the batter into prepared pan and cover with foil. Bake mochi one hour. Cool completely. Cut mochi with a plastic knife.

27324-99

Chien doi

Dough:
3³/₄ c. mochiko
1¹/₂ c. dark brown sugar
1¹/₄ c. hot water
1 tsp. sherry
Filling:
¹/₂ c. chopped roasted peanuts
¹/₂ c. shredded coconut
3 T. white sugar
¹/₄ c. toasted sesame seeds
oil for deep frying

Place mochiko in to large mixing bowl. In a small bowl, dissolve brown sugar in hot water. Stir sugar water into mochiko. Make a stiff dough. Do not over work dough. Add sherry and mix. Shape dough into 1¹/₂ inch diameter rolls. Cut rolls into ¹/₂ inch slices. Flatten each piece and place 1 T. of filling into center of dough piece. Bring up edges and pinch together to seal. Roll balls in sesame seeds. Heat oil to 350°. Fry balls until golden brown. If you want hollow chien doi - press balls against side of pan while frying so balls will expand.

Filling

¹/₂ c. chopped roasted peanuts
¹/₂ c. shredded coconut
3 T. white sugar

Combine the peanuts, coconut and white sugar in a bowl.

CHINESE CRISPY ORANGE COOKIES

1/2 c. mochiko
1 c. flour
1/2 c. butter
3/8 c. sugar
1 egg, separated
1/2 c. brown sugar
Grated rind of 1 large orange

Preheat oven to 350°. Grease cookie sheets. Sift flour and mochiko into a mixing bowl. Cut in the butter until the mixture resembles fine bread crumbs. Add sugar, orange rind and egg yolk. Mix well. Knead dough until it is smooth. Wrap in foil and refrigerate for 1/2 hour. Roll dough out into a 12 inch square. Brush lightly with beaten egg white; sprinkle with brown sugar. Fold corners to center. Form into a ball and knead lightly. Divide dough in half and roll each half into a 9 inch roll. Cut each roll into 1/2 inch thick slices. Place slices on cookie sheets and bake for 20 minutes. Cool.

CHOCOLATE MOCHI

2 c. mochiko
2 c. white sugar
1 T. baking soda
1/2 c. melted butter or margarine
1 c. semi-sweet chocolate chips
2 cans of 12 oz. each evaporated milk
2 beaten eggs
2 tsp. vanilla

Preheat oven to 350°. Grease a 9 x 13-inch pan. Sift mochiko, sugar and baking soda into a large mixing bowl. Melt butter or margarine with the chocolate chips. Be careful not to burn. Mix milk, eggs and vanilla together in a small mixing bowl. Add chocolate mixture to milk mixture and stir. Pour liquid mixture into dry ingredients and stir until smooth. Pour batter into prepared pan. Bake for 55 minutes. Cool completely before cutting.

Patricia Smith

27324-99

Chocolate mochi 2

2 c. mochiko
2 eggs
1/4 c. butter
1 3/4 c. white sugar
3 T. cocoa
4 tsp. baking soda
1 can coconut milk
1 can evaporated milk

Preheat oven to 350°. Melt butter in 9 x 13-inch pan. Set aside. Beat eggs with sugar in a large mixing bowl. Add coconut milk and evaporated milk. Mix well. Add mochiko, baking soda and cocoa to milk mixture. Mix until smooth. Pour into prepared pan and bake for 1 hour. Cool completely before cutting. Cut with plastic knife.

Mary Lou Nash

Cocoa mochi

1-lb. box mochiko
1 3/4 c. white sugar
3 T. cocoa powder
1 T. baking soda
2 beaten eggs
12 oz. can evaporated milk
1 can coconut milk
1 tsp. vanilla
1/4 c. melted butter

Preheat oven to 350°. Grease and flour a 9 x 13-inch pan. Sift mochiko, sugar, cocoa and baking soda into a large mixing bowl. Add eggs, milk, butter and vanilla. Mix until batter is smooth. Pour batter into prepared pan. Bake for 1 hour and 10 minutes. Cool completely and cut with a plastic knife.

Bertha Newsome

Coconut Azuki Mochi

1½ lb. mochiko
2¼ c. brown sugar
1 c. water
1 can coconut milk
1 tsp. baking soda
1 can tsubushian
2 T. sesame seeds

Preheat oven to 350°. Grease a 9 x 13-inch pan. Sift mochiko, sugar and baking soda together into a large mixing bowl. Add coconut milk, water and tsubushian and mix until smooth. Pour batter into prepared pan. Sprinkle sesame seeds on top of batter. Bake for 1 hour. Remove from oven and cool.

Coconut Azuki Mochi 2

2½ pkg. mochiko - 10 oz. each
2¼ c. brown sugar
1 can coconut milk
1 c. water
1 tsp. baking soda
1 can tsubushian
1 T. sesame seeds

Preheat oven to 350°. Grease a 9 x 13-inch pan. Mix mochiko, sugar, coconut milk, water, baking soda and tsubushian together in a large mixing bowl. Pour batter into prepared pan. Sprinkle top with sesame seeds. Bake for 1 hour. Cool completely before cutting.

27324-99

COCONUT MOCHI

1 lb. mochiko
2¼ c. white sugar
1 tsp. baking powder
1 can coconut milk
1 can water
1 tsp. coconut or vanilla extract
potato or cornstarch to dust

Preheat oven to 350°. Grease a 9 x 13-inch pan. In a large mixing bowl, stir the mochiko, sugar and baking powder together. Add coconut milk, water and extract to flour mixture. Stir until batter is smooth. Pour batter into pan. Cover tightly with foil. Bake for 1 hour. Remove from oven and let cool for 5 minutes. Carefully remove foil. Let mochi cool completely before cutting. Dust with potato or cornstarch.

COCONUT MOCHI 2

3 c. mochiko
½ tsp. baking powder
¼ tsp. salt
1 c. dark brown sugar
1 can coconut milk
½ c. water
½ tsp. vanilla
2 T. sesame seeds
potato or cornstarch for dusting

Preheat oven to 350°. Grease a 9 x 13-inch pan. Mix the mochiko, baking powder, salt and brown sugar together. Stir in coconut milk, water and vanilla. Mix until batter is smooth. Pour into prepared pan. Sprinkle with sesame seeds. Bake for 45 minutes. Cool completely. Cut into strips. Dust pieces with potato or cornstarch.

Mary Lou Nash

COCONUT MOCHI BALL WITH PEANUT BUTTER

1 c. mochiko
1/4 tsp. salt
1/4 c. white sugar
1/2 c. coconut milk
1/2 c. shredded coconut flakes
1/2 c. honey
potato starch for dusting
3/4 c. chunky peanut butter
6 T. brown sugar

In a small bowl mix together the peanut butter and brown sugar. Set filling aside for later use. In a medium mixing bowl, stir together the mochiko, sugar and salt. Add the coconut milk and mix until a soft dough forms. Knead dough for 2 minutes. Set up a steamer pot and basket. Line the basket with cheese cloth. Pour the dough on to the cheese cloth and wrap. Steam dough for 25 minutes. Pour the dough out on to a flat surface that has been dusted with potato starch. Let dough cool for several minutes. Knead dough for 2 minutes until shiny and smooth. Roll dough into a 8 inch log. Cut log into 8 pieces. Flatten each piece into a circle. Place 1 T. of peanut filling onto each circle. Fold up edges and pinch to seal. Drizzle the mochi with honey and roll in coconut flakes.

COCONUT NANTU

5 c. mochiko
3 c. brown sugar
1 tsp. baking soda
1 tsp. vanilla
2 1/2 c. water
1 can coconut milk

Preheat oven to 350°. Grease and flour a 9 x 13-inch pan. Stir the mochiko, sugar and baking soda together in a large mixing bowl. Add water, coconut milk and vanilla to flour mixture. Stir until smooth. Pour batter into prepared pan. Bake for 1 hour. Remove from oven and cool.

27324-99

Coconut Nantu 2

4 c. mochiko
½ pkg. haupia mix
3 c. water
1¾ c. white sugar
½ tsp. salt
kinako

Mix haupia mix with water in a large mixing bowl. Add mochiko and salt to liquid and blend well. Pour dough into a double layered cheesecloth and steam for 45 minutes. Pour hot dough into a mixing bowl and add sugar. Beat until dough is smooth. Sift kinako into a 9 x 13-inch pan. Pour mochi into pan and let cool for several hours. Sprinkle more kinako on top of coconut nantu before cutting.

Coconut Pancakes

1 ½ c. mochiko
2 c. coconut milk
3 eggs, beaten
½ c. white sugar
½ tsp. salt
¾ c. sweetened coconut flakes
red and green food coloring
oil

Place coconut milk, mochiko, eggs, sugar and salt in mixing bowl and mix until batter is smooth. Add ½ c. of coconut and stir. Divide batter in to 3 bowls. Add 6 drops of red food coloring in first bowl, 6 drops of green coloring in second bowl and leave third bowl plain. Mix each batters. Pour batters in to 6 inch rounds on a griddle or omelette pan and cook like normal pancakes. After flipping pancakes and cooking briefly on second side, remove from pan and roll. Place on a warm platter. Inter mix the colored pancakes on the platter. Sprinkle with remaining coconut.

Coconut Rice Cakes

1 c. mochiko
1/4 tsp. salt
1/4 c. packed light brown sugar
1/2 c. coconut flakes
1/2 c. coconut milk
potato starch
honey

In a medium bowl, stir together mochiko, sugar and salt. Add coconut milk to flour mixture and mix until smooth. This will form a soft dough. Set up a steamer pot with basket. Line the basket with cheese cloth. Pour dough onto the cheese cloth and cover. Steam dough for 20 to 25 minutes. Pour dough onto a flat surface that has been dusted with potato starch. Let dough cool for several minutes. Knead dough for several minutes until dough is smooth. Roll dough into an 8 inch log and cut into 8 pieces. Dust pieces with potato starch to prevent sticking. Form pieces into little oval mounds and place on a dusted surface. Drizzle honey over pieces then roll pieces in coconut flakes. Eat while fresh for best quality.

Custard Mochi

2 c. mochiko
1 1/2 c. white sugar
2 tsp. baking powder
1/2 c. butter
2 beaten eggs
4 c. milk
2 tsp. vanilla

Preheat oven to 350°. Grease a 9 x 13-inch pan. Cream sugar and butter together. Beat in one egg at a time. Add mochiko, baking powder, milk and vanilla. Mix until batter is smooth. Pour into prepared pan. Bake for 1 hour or until mochi is set. Cool for 2 hours before cutting.

Michelle Abreu

27324-99

Custard mochi II

4 c. mochiko
2½ c. white sugar
4 c. milk
4 eggs
3 tsp. baking powder
2 tsp. vanilla
½ c. melted butter

Preheat oven to 325°. Grease and flour a 9 x 13-inch pan. In a large mixing bowl, mix together the mochiko, sugar, baking powder, milk and the eggs. Add the vanilla and butter. Mix batter until smooth. Pour batter into prepared baking pan. Bake for 1 hour and 20 minutes. Cool. Slice with a plastic knife.

Daifuku

1 c. mochiko
½ c. white sugar
1 c. boiling water
1 can tsubushian
potato starch for dusting

Dissolve sugar in boiling water. Pour sugar water into mochiko and mix well. Bring a steamer pot of water to a boil. Place a damp cheesecloth that has been doubled onto steamer basket. Pour dough onto cheesecloth and wrap. Place basket in pot of simmering water and steam for 25 minutes. Carefully lift basket out of pot and unwrap cheesecloth. Pour dough on to dusted work surface. Cool five minutes. Break dough into golf ball size pieces and flatten in palm of hand leaving a shallow well in center. Roll 1 T. of of bean paste into a ball and place in center of mochi. Bring up sides and pinch patties to seal. Dust with potato starch.

Dau lau

2 c. mochiko
1 c. water
³/₄ c. shredded coconut
³/₄ c. sugar
³/₄ c. roasted unsalted peanuts, chopped fine
¹/₃ c. sesame seeds, toasted

Bring 6 c. of water to boil in large pot. Mix mochiko and water together to form a dough. Pinch pieces of dough to make balls the size of large walnuts. Drop balls into boiling water. Boil for 10 minutes. Balls will float to the top when done. Remove from water and drain. In a mixing bowl, combine coconut, sugar, peanuts and sesame seeds. Roll mochi balls in this mixture while still warm.

Easy chi chi dango

4 c. mochiko
2¹/₂ c. white sugar
¹/₂ tsp. baking powder
1 can coconut milk
2 c. water
red food coloring
potato or cornstarch

Preheat oven to 325°. Grease a 9 x 13-inch pan. Stir mochiko, sugar and baking powder together, in a large mixing bowl. Add coconut milk, water and red food coloring and mix till smooth. Pour batter into prepared pan and bake for 1 hour. Turn off oven and leave mochi in for an additional 15 minutes. Cool. Cut into small rectangular pieces with a plastic knife. Dust pieces with potato or corn starch.

27324-99

Filipino Tupig

1 lb. mochiko
1 c. raw brown sugar
2 c. sweetened coconut flakes
2 c. coconut milk
1 T. sugar
1½ Tbsp. water
18 banana or ti leaves
oil

Preheat oven to 375°. Mix mochiko, brown sugar and coconut flakes together in a large mixing bowl. Gradually add coconut milk. Stir until well blended. In a small pot, add 1 T. sugar and ½ T. of water. Bring to boil for 1 minute. Sugar will turn brown with a slightly burnt smell. Remove pot from heat and add 1 T. of water. Stir. Add to batter and mix well. This will add color and a caramel flavor to batter. Prepare leaves: Cut leaves in 6 x 8 inch pieces. Wash and dry leaves. Oil leaf and place 1 T.. of batter approximately 1 inch from bottom and in center of leaf. Spread batter out into a 5 inch strip. There should be be an inch border on each side. Score the leaf with a knife where the 1 inch border is. Fold leaf inwards towards batter. Start to roll the leaf up until a small tube is formed. Place rolls on a baking dish and bake for 40 minutes. Turn once after 20 minutes. Serve hot or cold.

FIRNEE

5 tsp. mochiko
2 c. plus 3 T. milk
1/8 tsp. cardamon seeds
1/4 c. white sugar
1 T. chopped pistachios

Put mochiko in a bowl and slowly add the 3 T. of milk. Mix into a smooth paste. In a sauce pan, boil the 2 c. of milk over a medium-low flame. Crush the cardamon seeds and add them to the milk. Soon as the milk begins to boil and rise remove from the heat. Add the paste and stir until paste has dissolved. Place pan over low heat and bring mixture to a simmer. Simmer for 15 minutes. Stir frequently. Remove from heat and pour mixture into 4 bowls and cool. Sprinkle pistachios over the top of firnee and refrigerate. Chill several hours before serving.

FRIED MOCHI WITH HONEY

1 pkg. mochiko - 10 oz.
1/2 tsp. salt
1 c. water
1/4 c. dried Chinese red dates
3/4 c. honey
1 tsp. cinnamon
oil

Combine 2 c. mochiko and salt. Add water and mix thoroughly. Flour hands with remaining mochiko and form dough into 1 inch balls. Flatten balls until you have little cakes 2 inches in diameter. Seed and slice dates. Press slivers of dates into dough making a flower design. Fry mochi in a frying pan with 1/4 inch of oil. After 1 minute turn mochi over and fry second side. Mochi should be brown in color. Place mochi in an air tight container. Drizzle warmed honey and cinnamon over mochi. Cover container. Let stand for about a 1/2 hour before eating.

27324-99

GAO

6 c. mochiko
1 lb. brown sugar
1/2 tsp. baking powder
1/4 tsp. vanilla
2 can coconut milk - add enough water to make 4 cups liquid
1 lb. cooked yams mashed
sesame seeds

Preheat oven to 350°. Grease and foil line a 9 x 13-inch pan. Heat milk over double boiler. Dissolve brown sugar in hot milk. Add mochiko and yams alternately, while stirring. Add baking powder and vanilla and mix until smooth. Spread mixture into prepared pan. Cover tightly with foil. Place pan on top rack and a second pan with water on lower rack. Bake 2 hours. Let gau stand 24 hours before cutting.

GAO WITH YAMS

2 pkgs. of mochiko, 10 oz. each
1 lb. box dark brown sugar
1/3 c. grated coconut
2 T. oil
1/2 c. water
1 lb. can yams
1 tsp. sesame seeds
1 dried red date - hung jo

Preheat oven to 375°. Grease and line a round casserole dish with ti leaves. Mix sugar, mashed yams and coconut in a mixing bowl. Add oil, water, liquid from yams and mochiko and mix well. Pour batter into prepared pan. Place date in center. Sprinkle the top with sesame seeds. Cover pan tightly with foil. Bake bake for 1 hour and 45 minutes up till 2 hours. Mochi should be set. Cool uncovered overnight. Be careful removing foil - steam is very hot.

GOMA MOCHI

1 lb. box mochiko
1¼ c. white sugar
1¾ c. water
1 T. baking soda
1 pkg. black goma seeds or black sesame seeds
oil for frying

Heat oil to 350° in deep fryer. Sift mochiko, white sugar and baking soda into a large mixing bowl. Add water and seeds. Roll dough into walnut size balls and deep fry until golden brown.

GUINATAAN

2 cans of coconut milk
1 c. mochiko
1 c. water
½ c. white sugar
2 c. cooked yams or sweet potatoes
2 c. cooked taro
2 pcs. ripe bananas

Cut yams or potatoes and taro into ½ inch cubes. Cut bananas into ½ inch slices. Mix mochiko and ½ c. of coconut milk together. It will form a stiff dough. Shape dough into walnut size balls and place on a piece of wax paper. In a sauce pan bring remaining coconut milk, water and sugar to a simmer. Cook over a medium heat for 10 minutes, stirring occasionally. Add yams and mochi balls to sauce pan and cook 10 more minutes. Add taro and cooked for 15 minutes more or desired consistency. Remove from heat. Stir in banana. Cool slightly.

27324-99

Guinataan Rice with Corn

½ c. mochi gome
5 c. coconut milk
1 c. coconut kernels
1 tsp. salt
1 c. coconut cream
½ to 1 c. white sugar

Wash the mochi gome. Put the mochi gome and coconut milk into a sauce pan and bring to a boil. Turn down heat and simmer for 20 minutes. Add corn, salt and ½ c. sugar to rice and stir. Continue to cook until rice is soft. Add more sugar if you want guinataan sweeter. Serve warm topped with coconut cream.

Haupia Coconut Mochi

2 lbs. mochiko
2½ c. sugar
½ c. powdered milk
2 pkgs. haupia mix
8 T. butter
4 T. margarine
6 c. water
1 c. chopped macadamia nuts
½ c. shredded sweetened coconut
potato starch or cornstarch to dust

Preheat oven to 375°. Grease a 9 x 13-inch pan. Cream butter, margarine and sugar in a large mixing bowl. Add mochiko, haupia mix and powdered milk. Slowly add water to mixture. Mix until batter is smooth. Add nuts and coconut. Mix. Pour batter into prepared pan. Bake for 1 hour. Remove from oven and cool completely. Cut. Dust pieces of mochi with potato starch or corn starch.

INDIAN RICE PUDDING

2½ c. milk
½ c. white sugar
½ c. mochiko
2 tsp. chopped pistachios
2 tsp. slivered almonds
½ tsp. rose water or vanilla

Bring milk to boil in a heavy sauce pan. Lower heat. Add sugar and stir until dissolved. Gradually add mochiko. Stir constantly. Add nuts. Keep on stirring until mixture thickens. Remove from heat and add rose water or vanilla. Pour mixture into serving dish and allow to cool.

INDIAN RICE PUDDING II

2½ c. milk
½ c. sugar
½ c. mochiko
2 tsp. chopped pistachios
2 tsp. almonds, blanched and slivered
½ tsp. rose water
½ c. chopped dates or raisins

Bring the milk to a boil in a heavy saucepan. Lower heat and allow milk to simmer. Stir in sugar and then gradually add the mochiko. Stir mixture constantly or it will burn. Add almonds, pistachios and dates. Allow pudding to thicken. Remove from heat and stir in the rose water. Pour pudding into a serving bowl and cool. The pudding should be served cold.

27324-99

INDIAN TEETHING CAKE

1 c. mochiko
1 c. flour
1/2 tsp. baking soda
1/4 tsp. salt
1 T. Light sesame oil or vegetable oil
1 c. sweetened, shredded coconut
4 c. coconut milk
1/2 c. palm sugar or cane sugar if palm not available
2/3 c. water
1 T. white sugar

Mix flour, mochiko, salt and baking soda together in a large mixing bowl. Add water a little at a time to form a dough. Rub your hands with the oil and knead the dough until it is smooth. In a small bowl, mix together the sugar and coconut. Set aside. Pull off pieces of dough and flatten into a circle. Place a teaspoon of the coconut mixture in center of dough. Pull up sides of dough and form into a ball. Bring the coconut milk and 1 T. of sugar to a boil in a pot. Lower heat. Simmer. Drop dough balls into pot. Balls will sink. Stir gently to prevent sticking to bottom of pot. Balls will rise to top and float. Cook for an additional 10 minutes. Serve hot or cold with coconut liquid.

INSTANT MOCHI

1 lb. box mochiko
3 c. water
1 c. red label Karo syrup
red food coloring
potato starch

Place water and Karo syrup into a large saucepan and bring to a boil. Lower heat and add several drops of food coloring. Pour mochiko into mixture and stir. Keep stirring for approximately 5 minutes. Remove from heat. Cool until you can handle warm dough. Scoop mochi out by tablespoonfuls. Flatten into patties and dust with potato starch to prevent sticking.

Ip CHAI

1 lb. mochiko
½ c. chopped roasted peanuts
1 c. shredded coconut
1 tsp. toasted sesame seeds
4 blocks of wong tong - Chinese brown sugar
1½ c. water
½ inch strips of ti leaves
oil

Mix mochiko and approximately ½ cup water in a mixing bowl to form a stiff dough. Gradually add water as needed. Knead dough for 1 to 2 minutes. Let dough rest while preparing filling. Combine peanuts, coconut, sesame seeds and wong tong in a small bowl. Mix until well blended. Mixture will be dry. Divide dough into 20 pieces. Approximately the size of a walnut. Flatten each piece into a 3 inch diameter circle. Put 1 teaspoon of filling in center of dough and bring up edges to encase. Pinch dough to seal ball. Wrap each ball in an oiled piece of ti leaf. Place ball on an oiled steamer rack and steam for 25 minutes.

Ip JAI

⅔ c. shredded coconut
⅓ c. chopped roasted peanuts
1½ tsp. toasted sesame seeds
4 tsp. white sugar
2 c. mochiko
¾ c. to 1 c. water
5 large ti leaves or 1 banana leaf cut into 3 x 4 inch pieces. oil to
    grease leaves

Combine coconut, peanuts, sesame seeds and sugar in a small bowl. In a larger mixing bowl, combine mochiko and water. Make into a slightly crumbly dough. Divide dough into 12 portions. Press each dough into a circular shape. Approximately 3 inches in diameter. Place 1 tablespoon of filling in center of dough. Bring up edges and pinch to seal. Wrap each ball in a piece of oiled leaf and place in an oiled pan. Place pan in a large steamer pot and steam for 20 minutes.

27324-99

JELLO MOCHI

2 pkgs. mochiko - 10 oz. each
2 pkgs. Jello any flavor - 3 oz. each
2 cans soda water - same flavor as Jello
2 c. white sugar
3 tsp. baking powder
3 eggs, beaten
½ c. butter, melted
kinako or katakuri

Preheat oven to 350°. Grease a 9 x 13-inch pan and line it with wax paper. Combine mochiko, Jello, sugar and baking powder in large mixing bowl. Add unchilled soda water, eggs and butter. Mix well. Pour batter into prepared pan and bake for 1 hour. Cool, cut and roll mochi in kinako or katakuri.

KANOM BAH BIN
(Thai coconut cake)

1½ c. mochiko
1 c. sugar
¼ tsp. salt
1 egg
2 c. shredded coconut
1 c. water with 1 tsp. vanilla added
2-3 T. peanut oil

In a large mixing bowl, stir the mochiko, salt and sugar together. Beat the egg and add it to the flour mixture. Knead mixture. Add the shredded coconut and a little bit bit of the scented water. Knead the dough. Keep on adding water a little at a time. Blend mixture until smooth. Heat a griddle on the stove. Grease the surface with the peanut oil. Drop mixture onto the hot griddle, molding them into small, flat rounds. Grill on low to medium heat until golden brown. Flip over the cakes and grill the other side until golden brown. Serve warm

KASCARON

2 lb. box mochiko
1 c. sugar
4 c. sweetened shredded coconut
4 c. water
1/2 c. honey
oil for deep frying

Heat oil in a deep fryer. Mix mochiko, sugar coconut and water in a large mixing bowl. Mix all ingredients until a dough is formed. Shape dough into walnut size balls. Deep fry until golden brown. Remove from oil and drain on paper towels. Place mochi balls in a 9 x 13-inch pan and drizzle honey over balls.

KLEPON

(Indonesian Rice Balls)

1 1/2 c. mochiko
3/4 c. coconut milk
4 T. dark brown sugar
1 c. coconut flakes
1/4 tsp. salt
2 drops green food coloring

In a large bowl, mix together the mochiko and salt. Add the coconut milk and food coloring. Mix dough until smooth. Scoop dough out into walnut size balls. Roll into balls. Make an indent in each ball with your finger and place 1/4 tsp. full of brown sugar in hole. Pinch opening shut. Roll ball again until round. Prepare remaining balls and place on wax paper. Bring 8 cups of water to boil in a pot. When water begins to boil, drop several balls into pot at a time. When balls float to the surface, the mochi is cooked. Remove balls with a slotted spoon and drain. While balls are still hot roll them in the coconut flakes.

27324-99

Korean - injolmi

5 c. glutinous rice
1 T. salt
1/2 c. dried sweet beans
1/2 c. yellow bean flour
1/2 c. green bean flour

Wash and soak the glutinous rice and sweet beans over night. Drain. Put rice into a steamer basket lined with cheese cloth and steam for for at least an hour. Occasionally sprinkle rice with salted water and stir while steaming. While steaming the rice, rinse the sweet beans and rub off the bean skins completely. In another pot, steam the beans until tender. Place rice into a mixing bowl while still hot and mix with a dough hook. If you don't have a dough hook, pound the rice in a motar until dough is smooth. Cover dough and set aside. Mash the sweet beans and push through a sieve, making a purée. Wash the other beans and fry them in a pan or toast them in the oven for 15 minutes. Grind the beans into a powder and set aside. Wet your hands in water and remove the dough from its resting place. Put the dough onto a flat surface and flatten until it is about a half inch thick. Cut the dough into 1 1/2 inch rectangles and dip pieces into various bean flours. This is not a sweet dessert, more on the salty side.

KOREAN JU-AK

4 c. mochiko
2 c. warm water
2 c. chestnuts
1/2 c. dates
2 T. honey
1 c. white sugar
1/2 tsp. cinnamon
1/4 tsp. salt
sesame oil for frying

Boil chestnuts until cooked, approximately 25-30 minutes. Cool and peel the chestnuts. Remove the inner skin and mash. Add the honey and cinnamon. Mix well. Pinch off small amounts of paste and roll into balls the size of your thumb. Set aside. Seed and cut dates into lengthwise pieces about 1/15 inch wide. Mix mochiko, salt and warm water together. Knead for several minutes until dough is smooth. Pinch off dough into walnut size pieces. Roll pieces into a ball, then flatten. Place the chestnut ball in center of flattened dough ball. Fold the dough in half and pinch to seal. Press date threads onto outside of little pancakes. Put sesame oil into a frying pan and toast the little pancakes on both sides until brown. When done, sprinkle with sugar.

27324-99

Korean kang-jung

6 c. glutinous rice
2 c. honey
1 c. toasted sesame seeds
3 c. frying oil ⅔ c. rice wine
4½ T. white sugar
½ tsp. salt
15-20 walnut halves
¼ c. flour or potato starch

Soak glutinous rice for 3 days in water. Drain and rinse. Place rice in a grinder or food processor and grind all the rice into a powder. Mix the rice powder with ⅔ c. rice wine, 4½ T. sugar and ½ tsp. salt. A soft dough will form. Knead the dough for 2 minutes until smooth and shiny. Set up a steamer pot and basket. Line basket with cheese cloth. Place dough in center of lined basket cover with cheese cloth. Steam dough for 25 minutes. Pour dough out onto a dusted flat surface. Let cool for several minutes. Knead dough again while still warm. Flatten out dough until approximately ¼ to ⅓ inch thick. Cut dough into triangles. Leave dough out on counter to dry out or in a sunny area. It'll take several hours. Dip the dry triangles in oil and set aside. Set up a pan for deep frying these cookies. When the oil is hot drop oiled cookies into pan. Fry cookies until light golden brown. Drain cookies. Dip cookies into honey one at a time, sprinkle with the toasted sesame seeds and place a piece of walnut in the center.

KOREAN - SWEET RICE

5 c. glutinous rice
2 c. dark brown sugar
3 T. sesame oil
3 T. soy sauce
10 chestnuts
20 hung jo - red date
2 T. raisins
¼ c. pine nuts

Wash and soak glutinous rice over night. Drain rice and place rice into a cheesecloth in a steamer. Put the chestnuts on the rice and steam rice for approximately 45 minutes. While steaming rice, occasionally sprinkle rice with salt water and stir. Pit and cut the red dates into 4 pieces. Remove the tops of the pine nuts. Put red dates, pine nuts, raisins, sugar, sesame oil and soy sauce into a glass or metal mixing bowl. Add steamed rice and mix well. Place bowl into the steamer and steam for 20 minutes longer. Fluff up the rice every 5 minutes while steaming. After rice is fully cooked, spoon rice mixture into greased custard bowls or Jello molds. Pack rice tightly. Then turn rice molds upside down to remove the sweet rice. Serve hot or room temperature.

LAZY MAN'S CHI CHI DANGO

1 lb. box mochiko
3 c. white sugar
1 can coconut milk
2 c. water
red food coloring
potato starch or kinako

Preheat oven to 350°. Grease a 9 x 13-inch pan. Combine mochiko, sugar, coconut milk and water in a mixing bowl. Stir until smooth. Add several drops of food coloring to dough and mix. Dough should be pink. Pour dough into prepared pan. Cover pan securely with foil. Bake for 1 hour. Remove pan from oven. Cool for 5 minutes. Carefully remove foil. The steam will be very hot. Cool completely. Cut mochi with plastic knife. Roll pieces in potato starch or kinako.

27324-99

Lemon jello mochi

4 c. mochiko
3 tsp. baking powder
2 c. white sugar
2 boxes lemon Jello
½ c. melted butter or margarine
3 eggs beaten
2 cans 7-Up or Sprite
potato flour or cornstarch for dusting mochi

Preheat oven to 350°. Mix mochiko, baking powder, sugar and Jello together in a large mixing bowl. Add butter, eggs and 7 up or Sprite to the flour mixture. Mix by hand until smooth. Pour into a greased 9 x 13-inch pan. Bake for one hour. Remove and cool completely. Cut mochi into bit size pieces and dust with potato flour or cornstarch.

Malagkit na ubi

12 oz. Halayang Ubi - Purple yam found in Asian Stores
5 c. mochiko
1 tsp. baking soda
1 can coconut milk
1½ c. water
1 c. shredded coconut

Preheat oven to 350°. Grease a 9 x 13-inch pan and set aside. Mix mochiko, baking soda and shredded coconut together in a large mixing bowl. Add mashed yams, coconut milk and water to flour mixture. Mix well. Pour batter into a prepared pan and bake for 1 hour. Cool completely before cutting.

Mangoes and Mochi Rice

1 1/2 cup mochi gome - glutinous rice
1 1/2 c. coconut milk
1/2 c. white sugar
1/2 tsp. salt
5 ripe mangoes
4 T. coconut syrup or cream

Soak rice over night. Rinse rice and cook in rice cooker with 1 1/2 c. water. Boil the coconut milk until it is reduced to 1 cup. Add sugar and salt and simmer until sugar is dissolved. Add milk mixture to the warm sticky rice. Let rice stand for a 1/2 hour. Peel and cut mangoes in half. Remove seed and cut each mango half into 4 more slices. Cutting mango the long way, so the slices will be in strips. Place mochi rice on a platter and arrange mango slices around the sides of the rice. Drizzle coconut syrup over top and sides of rice.

Susan Phan

Microwave an Mochi

1 1/2 c. mochiko
1/2 c. white sugar
1 1/2 c. water
1 can Tsubushian
potato starch or cornstarch for dusting

Grease a microwavable tube pan or a 9 x 13-inch glass pan. Mix mochiko and sugar together. Pour water into dry mixture while stirring constantly. Pour mochi into prepared pan. Microwave on "HIGH" for seven minutes or until done. Cool. Pour mochi onto a board with potato starch. Divide mochi into fourteen pieces. Flatten each piece and fill with an. Bring mochi up and around the an and seal. Shape into patties. Dust patties with potato starch.

MICROWAVE CHI CHI DANGO

1 lb. box mochiko
2½ c. white sugar
1 tsp. vanilla
2 c. water
1 can coconut milk
red food coloring
potato starch or kinako

Grease a 9 x 13-inch glass pan or microwave dish. Mix mochiko, sugar, vanilla, water and coconut milk in a large mixing bowl. Add several drops of red food coloring to mixture. Stir until dough is smooth and light pink. Pour batter into pan and cover tightly with plastic wrap or lid. Microwave mochi on **high** for 5 minutes. Turn pan and microwave mochi on **medium** for 3 to 5 minutes more. Remove and let cool. Cut mochi with a plastic knife. Roll mochi in potato starch or kinako.

michelle abreu

MICROWAVE GAU

16 oz. pkg. wong tong - Chinese brown sugar
1 lb. mochiko
1 can coconut milk
2 c. boiling water
¼ c. vegetable oil or peanut oil
sesame seeds

Grease a microwave tube pan. Dissolve wong tong in boiling water. Place mochiko in a large mixing bowl. Gradually stir sugar water into mochiko. Add coconut milk and oil. Beat mixture until smooth. Pour batter into the prepared pan. Cover pan loosely with clear wrap. Microwave on **high** for 15 to 18 minutes. Remove pan from microwave. Carefully remove wrap from pan and sprinkle sesame seeds on top of gau. Let gau cool for at least 3 hours before cutting.

MOCHI BALLS WITH PEANUT BUTTER

2 c. mochiko
3 T. white sugar
1 T. margarine, melted
1/4 c. flour
1/2 c. boiling water
6 T. brown sugar
3/4 c. chunky peanut butter
powdered sugar

Mix mochiko, white sugar and margarine together in a mixing bowl. In another bowl mix flour with boiling water. Mix both mixtures together to form a dough. Knead. Gradually add 1/4 c. cold water to dough and continue to knead until dough is smooth. Roll dough into 12 to 15 balls. In a small mixing bowl, mix together brown sugar and peanut butter. Flatten mochi balls and place 1 tsp. of filling in center. Bring up sides to encase peanut butter filling. Arrange balls on a greased steamer rack and steam for 12 minutes. Remove balls and roll in powdered sugar.

Teresa Lam

MOCHI CAKE

1 box mochiko
2 1/2 c. white sugar
2 tsp. baking powder
5 beaten eggs
1/2 c. melted butter or margarine
3 c. milk
2 tsp. vanilla
1 tsp. lemon extract
1 c. shredded sweetened coconut

Preheat oven to 350°. Grease a 9 x 13-inch baking pan. Combine mochiko, sugar, shredded coconut and baking powder in a mixing bowl. Add eggs, butter, milk, vanilla and lemon extract to flour mixture and mix well. Pour batter into the pan. Bake for 1 hour. Cool for at least 2 hour. Cut with plastic knife.

27324-99

MOCHI GOME WITH AN

2 c. mochi rice - glutinous rice
1 c. water
1 c. Tsubushian or Koshian
Potato starch - Katakuriko

Grease a microwave bundt pan. Wash mochi rice and soak in water for two hours. Drain. Put rice and water into a food processor or blender and process until liquefied. Pour batter into pan. Microwave on "HIGH" for five to seven minutes. Cool. Place mochi on a board dusted with potato starch. Divide into twelve pieces. Flatten out each piece and put a tablespoon or tsubushian in the center. Pinch sides together to seal in. Dust with potato starch.

MOCHI GOME WITH COCONUT

½ lb. mochi rice - glutinous rice
1 can coconut milk
2 c. brown sugar
1 tsp. oil

Preheat oven to 350°. Grease a 9 x 13-inch pan. Rinse mochi rice. Put rice and an equal amount of water in rice cooker and steam like regular rice. Combine sugar and coconut milk in a saucepan and bring to a boil. Lower heat and simmer for 5 minutes. Divide syrup into two equal parts. Mix ½ of syrup with cooked rice. Pour rice mixture into prepared pan. Pour remaining syrup over mixture. Bake for 20 minutes. Cool completely before cutting.

MOCHI RICE WITH PURPLE RICE

2 c. mochi gome
2 T. purple rice or pirurutung
2 c. water
½ c. white sugar
1½ c. shredded coconut

Soak purple rice over night. Wash and drain mochi gome and place in a rice cooker. Drain purple rice and add to mochi gome. Add 2 c. water and stir. Turn on rice cooker and let it cook its' regular cycle. After rice cooker clicks off, add sugar and stir. Recover pot and let set for 15 minutes in its' own steam. Scoop rice out into walnut size balls. Roll balls in coconut and enjoy.

MOCHI SNOWBALLS

1 pkg. mochiko - 10 oz.
2 c. flour
1½ white sugar
½ tsp. salt
3 eggs, beaten
4 T. baking powder
1½ c. milk
oil
powder sugar for sprinkling

Heat oil to 350°in deep fryer. Mix mochiko, flour, sugar, baking powder and salt together in a large mixing bowl. Add milk and eggs and mix until well blended. Drop by tablespoon into hot oil and fry until golden brown. Sprinkle with powdered sugar while still warm.

27324-99

Nantuyinsu 1

4 c. mochiko
1 c. miso
1 c. water
1½ c. brown sugar
1 tsp. ground black pepper
¼ c. raw peanuts
2 ti leaves

Combine miso, brown sugar, water, mochiko and black pepper in a bowl and mix. Knead dough until it is smooth. Divide into 3 equal parts and shape each into a 5 x 8 x ¾ inch rectangle. Place each rectangle onto a piece of ti leaf. Decorate top with peanuts and the place rectangle on a steamer rack. Steam for 45 minutes or until soft. Cool and cut into 2½ x 1 inch strips.

Nantuyinsu 2

4 c. mochiko
1½ c. brown sugar
1 c. miso
1 c. water
1 tsp. ground black pepper
½ c. raw peanuts
2 ti leaves

Mix mochiko, sugar, miso, pepper, and water together in a large mixing bowl. Knead dough until smooth. Place ti leaves into a greased cake pan. Pat dough onto ti leaves to about ¾ inch thick. Sprinkle peanuts on top of dough. Place cake pan into a steamer and steam for 45 minutes or until soft. Cool and cut into pieces.

Nien Gao

1 lb. wong tong - Chinese brown sugar
1/2 c. raw brown sugar
2 1/2 c. hot water
1 lb. mochiko, sifted
1/4 c. oil
1 dried red date
2 tsp. toasted sesame seeds
6 ti leaves

Oil ti leaves and a 7 1/2 x 3 inch round pan. Line pan with ti leaves. Dissolve sugars in hot water. Cool. Gradually add mochiko. Stir in 1/4 c. oil and mix well. Pour batter into prepared pan. Place pan in large steamer and steam for 4 hours. Be sure to check steamer has water on bottom every hour. Remove gau when done and sprinkle with sesame seeds. Top with good luck date. Let stand 24 hours before cutting.

Ohagi

2 c. mochi rice
2 c. water
1 tsp. salt

Soak mochi rice in water overnight. Cook rice until tender. Cool slightly and then gently mash the rice. Rice will remain chunky. Roll rice into small balls about the size of a walnut. Coat rice balls with bean mixture.

bean mixture

1 can koshi or tsubushi an
1/2 c. white sugar

Combine koshi an and sugar in a saucepan and cook on low heat for 5 minutes. Cool.

27324-99

OKINAWAN MOCHI

4 c. mochiko
3 c. water
1³/₄ c. white sugar
½ tsp. salt
kinako
red food coloring - optional

Mix mochiko, water and salt until smooth. Pour into double thickness cheese cloth and steam for 50 minutes. Pour steamed mochi immediately into a mixing bowl and add sugar. The hot mochi will dissolve sugar. Beat until sugar is well incorporated. Add food coloring at this time if desired. Dust a 9 x 13-inch pan with kinako. Pour mochi into pan and spread out. Cool overnight or for at least 6 hours. Cover with a dry dish towel. Do not use Saran wrap. Cut and dust with kinako.

OKINAWAN PURPLE POTATO MOCHI

1 box mochiko
1¼ cup brown sugar
1½ cup hot water
4 medium size okinawan potatoes
1 small can condensed sweetened milk
oil for deep frying

Boil potatoes for 20 to 30 minutes. Potatoes should be soft. Cool. Peel potatoes and mash. Add sweeten condensed milk. If you want filling sweeter, add a little sugar. Mix mixture until all lumps are mashed. Dissolve brown sugar in the hot water. Cool. Put mochiko in a large bowl. Add sugar water slowly while beating mochiko. Add enough water to mochiko to form a stiff dough. Scoop and form dough into walnut size balls. Flatten balls. Place a teaspoon of sweet potato filling on center of each flattened ball. Bring dough up and around the filling. Pinch the ends to seal. Drop balls into preheated oil and fry until golden brown. Drain and serve.

OKINAWAN YAM MOCHI

2 lb. mochiko
1½ c. white sugar
¼ tsp. salt
2 eggs, beaten
2 medium sweet potatoes
6 medium yams
oil

Boil sweet potatoes and yams until they are soft. Peel and mash together. Add mochiko and eggs to yam mixture and mix until dough becomes manageable and firm. Add sugar and salt gradually. Mix thoroughly. Form dough into oblong shapes, 2½ inches long and 1 inch in diameter. Deep fry mochi in oil that has been heated to 375°. Mochi is done when they float and are golden brown in color. Drain and cool before eating.

27324-99

ORANGE SHAPED CAKES

2 c. mochiko
1 tsp. baking powder
1/2 tsp. salt
1/2 c. sugar
2 med. potatoes, boiled, peeled and mashed
1/2 c. boiling water
1/2 c. toasted sesame seeds
oil for deep frying

Mix together, the mochiko, baking powder, salt, sugar and mashed potatoes in a large mixing bowl. Gradually add boiling water. Mix until a soft dough forms. Knead for several minutes until smooth. Make a ball with 2 tablespoons of the dough. Flatten ball into a 3 inch circle. Place a teaspoon of filling mixture into center of dough and pull up sides around filling. Reshape into a ball. Roll balls in toasted sesame seeds. Fry balls in hot oil until golden brown, approximately 10 minutes. Drain on paper towels and serve warm.

Filling

3/4 c. mung beans
3/4 c. water
1/2 c. white sugar

Rinse mung beans under cold water. Place beans and water in a pot and bring to boil. Cover the pan and reduce the heat. Simmer for 30 minutes. When the beans are tender and the water is cooked away, remove from heat. Mash beans with the sugar and set aside for use.

OSHIRUKU

1 c. dry Azuki beans
1/4 tsp. salt
1 3/4 c. white sugar
5 c. water
12 pieces Komochi - found in Asian stores

Clean and rinse beans. Put beans in a pot and cover with water and bring to a boil. As soon as water starts to boil remove pot from stove and drain. Add five cups of water to pot and cook beans at a simmer for two hours. When beans are tender add additional water to make five cups in pot. Add sugar and salt. Stir. Cook bean mixture for ten more minutes or until sugar is dissolved. Toast Komochi on griddle. Place two pieces in each bowl and cover with cooked Azuki beans.

PALITAW

2 c. mochiko
2 T. white sugar
3/4 c. water
2 1/2 c. sweetened shredded coconut
3 droops of red food coloring

Mix mochiko, 1 T. of sugar and water until a stiff dough is formed. Roll into walnut size balls. Drop several at a time into boiling water. Cook until balls float to the top of the pot. Remove and drain. Immediately sprinkle with remaining sugar and roll into colored coconut.

27324-99

Paridosdos

5 fresh yams
8 ripe bananas
2 lb. box mochiko
2 cans of coconut milk
1 1/2 c. white sugar
1 1/2 to 2 c. water
3 T. vanilla

Peel and cut yams into 1/2 inch pieces. Soak in water. Peel and cut bananas cross wise into 1/4 inch thick pieces. Set aside. Mix mochiko and 1 1/2 c. water. Make a semi-stiff dough. Add more water if needed. You should be able to roll dough into walnut size balls with out them sticking together. Place balls on dusted wax paper until all balls are rolled. In a large pot, add coconut milk with 2 c. water. Boil for 8 minutes. Reduce heat and simmer for 15 minutes longer. Add 8 c. water, sugar and vanilla. Continue to simmer 10 more minutes. Add yams and cook until half cooked. Add mochi balls and banana. Cook until mochi balls float to the top. Serve in a bowl. Refrigerate uneaten portion.

Peanut Rice Cakes - Rakkasei no Mochi

1 c. mochiko
1/4 tsp. salt
1/4 c. packed light brown sugar
1/3 c. cocktail peanuts
1/2 c. water
 1/2 c. kinako
honey
potato starch for dusting

In a food processor or blender, grind peanuts until it forms a paste. Add water and blend until smooth. Mix peanut mixture with mochiko, salt and brown sugar in a medium size mixing bowl. A soft dough will form. Knead dough for a minute. Set up a steamer pot with basket. Line basket with cheese cloth. Pour dough onto cheese cloth and flatten to about 1/2 inch thick. Cover and steam for 20 minutes. After 20 minutes, lift dough out of pot and place on a flat surface that has been dusted with the potato starch. Let cool for several minutes until you can handle it with out burning your hands. Knead dough for 2 minutes until it is shiny and smooth. Roll dough into an 8 inch log. Cut log into 8 pieces. Dust with additional potato starch to prevent sticking. Place pieces on to a dish. Coat mochi with honey. Roll pieces in kinako. It is best to eat mochi the same day that it is made.

Peche Peche

1/4 c. Pirurutung - purple rice found in China town
2 c. mochi rice
2 c. water
1/2 c. white sugar
1 1/2 c. sweetened shredded coconut

Soak pirurutung overnight. Rinse mochi rice and drain. Put mochi rice, pirurutung and water into a sauce pan and cook for twenty minutes - covered. Add sugar and mix well. Mixture should still be wet. Cover and continue to cook until rice is tender. Cool slightly. Scoop out rice and form into balls. Roll balls in the shredded coconut.

27324-99

PECHE PECHE II

2 c. mochi gome
2 T. pirurutung or purple rice (found in china town)
2 c. water
1/2 c. white sugar
1 1/2 c. shredded coconut

Soak purple rice over night. Wash and drain the 2 cups of mochi gome. Put the mochi gome and drain purple rice into a rice cooker pot. Add 2 cups of water and turn on rice cooker. After 20 minutes stir the sugar into the rice and recover the pot. Let rice cooker sit for at least 15 minutes after done cooking. Do not lift the lid. Scoop the rice and roll into 1 1/4 inch balls. Roll balls in shredded coconut. Best to eat warm.

POI COCONUT MOCHI

4 1/2 c. mochiko
1 1/2 c. white sugar
3 c. poi - already prepared
1 c. water
4 oz. sesame seeds
1 1/2 c. shredded sweetened coconut

Mix mochiko, sugar, coconut and sesame seeds together. Add water and poi to flour mixture. Blend well. Drop dough by tablespoonful into oil that has been heated to 375°. Fry until golden brown. Drain on paper towel. Cool.

POI MOCHI

1 lb. box mochiko
1 c. white sugar
1/2 tsp. baking powder
1 tsp. vanilla
3/4 c. water
1 lb. fresh poi - not mixed

Mix mochiko, sugar and baking powder together. Add vanilla, water and poi to flour mixture and mix until dough is smooth. Drop dough by table-spoonful into oil that has been heated to 375°. Fry until golden brown. Cool.

Teresa Lam

POI MOCHI 2

1/2 c. mochiko
1 c. white sugar
1 1/4 c. flour
1 lb. fresh poi - not mixed
3/4 c. water
oil for deep frying

Mix mochiko, sugar and flour together. Add water and poi to flour mixture and mix until dough is smooth. Drop dough by tablespoonful into oil heated to 375°. Fry until golden brown. Cool.

PUMPKIN MOCHI

2 pkgs. mochiko - 10 oz. each
3/4 c. brown sugar
1 c. shredded pumpkin or squash
2 1/2 c. coconut milk
oil for deep frying

Mix mochiko, pumpkin and brown sugar together. Add coconut milk gradu-ally while stirring. Dough should be soft enough to form wet balls. Add more coconut milk if dough is to hard. Drop dough by tablespoonful into hot oil. Fry until golden brown.

27324-99

PUMPKIN MOCHI

5 c. mochiko
2 c. white sugar
½ tsp. cinnamon
1½ tsp. pumpkin pie spice
2 tsp. baking powder
¼ tsp. salt
2 tsp. vanilla
4 eggs, beaten
1 c. melted butter or margarine
14 oz. can condensed sweeten milk
1 large 29 oz. can of solid pack pumpkin

Preheat oven to 350°. In a large mixing bowl, mix together the mochiko, sugar, baking powder, spices and salt. In a separate mixing bowl, beat the eggs, butter, milk, vanilla and pumpkin together until smooth. Gradually add the dry ingredients to the pumpkin mixture. Mix until smooth. Pour mochi into a well greased 9 x 13-inch pan. Bake for 1 hour. Cool completely. Let sit for several hours before cutting. Cut into small squares with a plastic knife.

QUICK MOCHI

1 c. white sugar
2½ c. water
1 lb. box mochiko
¼ tsp. red food coloring
kinako or potato starch to dust

Bring sugar and water to a boil in a sauce pan. Lower heat and add mochiko all at once. Beat dough until shiny. Add a little hot water if dough is to hard. Remove from heat. Let cool slightly. Knead dough for 2 to 3 minutes. Spread dough out on dusted surface and let cool thoroughly. Cut into strip and dust with more kinako or potato starch.

Refrigerator mochi

10 oz. mochiko
1 c. water
1/4 c. evaporated milk
1 1/2 c. sugar
1/2 c. water
pink or green food coloring if desired
kinako or potato starch for dusting

Mix the mochiko, water and evaporated milk together. Place dough into
a cheesecloth and steam for 40 minutes. In a medium saucepan, mix the
sugar and 1/2 c. water together. Bring to a boil. Reduce heat and simmer
for 30 minutes. Add several drops of food coloring to syrup if desired.
Place steamed dough into a mixing bowl. Be careful, dough will be very
hot. Gradually add the syrup and knead. Mixers with dough hooks work
well. Pour dough into a lightly oiled 8 x 9 inch pan. Refrigerate overnight.
Slice and roll in potato starch or kinako.

Rice balls with kinako

1 c. mochi rice
1 c. rice
2 1/4 c. water
6 T. kinako
4 T. sugar

Wash and drain rices. Put rices in a rice cooker with water and let stand
for 1 hour. Turn on rice cooker after letting rice stand and cook like regular.
After rice is cooked and slightly cooled; shape rice into 10 balls. Combine
kinako with sugar and salt. Roll rice balls in this mixture.

27324-99

Sesame Seed Puffs

2 c. mochiko
1½ c. sweet potato, cooked and mashed
1 c. brown sugar
¼ c. water
½ c. sesame seeds
oil for deep frying
1 can red bean paste

Mix the mochiko and the sweet potato together in a large mixing bowl. In a saucepan, dissolve the brown sugar in the water. Bring sugar water to a rolling boil. Immediately add water to the flour mixture and stir until dough is firm. Knead dough for several minutes. Divide dough in half and separate each half into twelve portions. Roll each piece into a ball. Flatten each ball till it forms a three inch round. Place a teaspoon of filling on each round. Pull up sides of dough to enclose filling. Pinch ends to seal. Roll dough into a ball again. Repeat with the rest of the dough. Deep fry the mochi balls in oil that has been heated to 350°. Fry approximately for 8 minutes. Balls will be brown in color. Drain and cool for 5 minutes before serving.

Snowballs

1 pkg. mochiko - 10 oz.
2 c. flour
1½ c. white sugar
½ tsp. salt
3 T. baking powder
3 eggs
½ tsp. vanilla
1½ c. milk
oil for deep fat frying

Mix mochiko, flour, sugar, salt, baking powder, eggs, vanilla, and milk together. Drop by tablespoonful into hot oil. Fry until golden brown. Remove. Drain. Roll in additional sugar.

Song pyun tok

2 c. mochiko
1⅛ tsp. salt
¾ c. boiling water
3 T. prepared sesame seeds
3 T. white sugar
1 tsp. cold water
1 T. sesame oil

Bring a quart of water to boil. Mix 2 c. mochiko, 1 tsp. salt and ¾ c. boiling water in a mixing bowl. Knead dough until very smooth. Cover with damp cloth and set aside. Mix toasted sesame seeds, sugar, ⅛ tsp. salt and 1 tsp. cold water into a small bowl. Form dough into walnut size balls. Make a hole in ball and place ¼ to ½ tsp. of sesame mixture into each ball. Seal hole and make into a clam shape. Drop mochi into boiling water and stir. When mochi floats to surface it is done. Drain. Place cooked mochi in a bowl and sprinkle with 1 T. sesame oil.

Steamed manju

10 oz. mochiko
10 oz. flour
1½ c. water
1 can azuki or koshi an bean
banana or ti leaf

Mix mochiko, flour and water together. Knead dough for several minutes. Form dough into walnut size balls. Flatten and place ½ tsp. of bean in center. Fold dough up and around paste and pinch ends together. Place on a banana leaf seam side down in a steamer. Steam for ½ hour.

27324-99

STEAMED MOCHI RICE

1/2 lb. mochi rice
2 c. brown sugar
1 can frozen coconut milk
1 tsp. vanilla

Preheat oven to 350°. Soak the mochi rice overnight. Place mochi rice and an equal amount of water into a rice cooker and steam like normal rice. While the rice is steaming, place brown sugar, vanilla and coconut milk into a sauce pan and bring to a boil. Mix half of the coconut mixture with the mochi rice. Spread the mixture into a greased 9 x 13-inch pan. Pour the rest of the milk over the mochi rice and bake for fifteen to twenty minutes. Mochi should be dry and lightly browned.

STEAMED THAI MOCHI

1 lb. mochi rice
2/3 c. white sugar or palm sugar
2 1/2 coconut milk

Soak mochi rice overnight. When ready to cook, drain and steam the rice with an equal amount of water in a rice cooker. While the mochi rice is steaming, place coconut milk and sugar in a sauce pan and bring it to a boil. Soon as the rice cooker clicks off, remove the rice. The rice will still be wet and soft. Place steamed mochi rice into coconut milk mixture and simmer until liquid is absorbed. Pour rice onto a serving plate. Flatten to about an inch thick. Let it cool. Cut into squares.

STICKY RICE WITH BANANAS

3 c. cooked mochi rice
1/4 c. brown sugar
1 c. coconut milk
6 ripe bananas
banana or ti leaves cut into 6 inch squares

Combine coconut milk and sugar in sauce pan and cook on medium low heat until sugar is dissolved. Rinse mochi rice and add to milk mixture. Cook until mixture thickens. Stir constantly. Be careful not to burn mochi rice. Place a layer of mochi rice on to a piece of banana or ti leaf. Mochi rice should be approximately 1/2 inch thick. Leave a 2 inch border around leaf. Place a 1 inch strip of banana on top of mochi rice. Pull up two opposite sides of banana leaf. The mochi rice will spread around the banana. Fold under extra part of leaf. Place on a steamer rack and steam for 25 minutes.

STRAWBERRY MOCHI

20 oz. mochiko
2 pkgs. strawberry Jello
2 c. white sugar
3 tsp. baking powder
3 beaten eggs
2 cans strawberry soda - room temperature
1/2 c. melted butter
potato starch or kinako for dusting

Preheat oven to 350°. Combine mochiko, Jello, sugar and baking powder in a large mixing bowl. Add strawberry soda, eggs, and butter. Mix batter until smooth. Pour into a greased 9 x 13-inch pan. Bake for one hour. Cool. Cut and dust with potato starch or kinako.

27324-99

Suman

5 c. mochi rice
5 c. water
1 lb. box brown sugar
1 can coconut milk

Wash mochi rice. Place in rice cooker with 5 cups of water and cook like normal rice. Grease a 9 x 13-inch pan. Place coconut milk in a large sauce pan and simmer until milk start to curdle and an oil film forms on the top. Add brown sugar and boil for 5 minutes. Add cooked mochi rice and stir until well blended. Cook on low heat for another 5 minutes. Stir occasionally to prevent burning. Pour into prepared pan and pack. Cool. Cut into squares.

Sweet Potato Andagi

5 oz. mochiko
1/2 c. white sugar
1 large cooked sweet potato
oil for deep fat frying

Peel sweet potato and mash. Add sugar and mochiko. Knead into a dough. If dough is to stiff add a little water. Pat dough out on a piece of wax paper to about a half inch thick. Using a round cookie cutter dusted in mochiko, cut the dough into small rounds or any other shape you desire. Fry until golden brown.

Sweet Potato Mochi

1 lb. mochiko
1¼ c. brown sugar
1 tsp. baking soda
⅛ tsp. salt
1 can coconut milk
1¼ c. water
2 c. cooked and mashed sweet potato
1 T. black sesame seeds
kinako

Preheat oven to 350°. Grease a 9 x 13-inch pan. In a large mixing bowl, sift mochiko, baking soda, sugar and salt. Add coconut milk and water and mix well. Fold in sweet potatoes. Pour batter into prepared pan. Sprinkle top with sesame seeds and bake for 1 hour. Cool. Cut and roll pieces in kinako.

Sweet Potato Mochi 2

3½ c. sweet potato, mashed
½ tsp. salt
1 c. white sugar
2 c. mochiko
oil
1 c. kinako

Combine sweet potato, ¼ tsp. salt, ½ c. sugar and mochiko in a large mixing bowl. Mix well. If dough is to stiff add a little warm water. Form dough into small patties and deep fry until light brown. Drain. While warm roll into a mixture of 1 cup kinako, ½ c. sugar and ¼ tsp. salt.

27324-99

Taro mochi

1 box mochiko
1½ c. white sugar
1 c. brown sugar
1 tsp. baking powder
½ c. butter or margarine
5 beaten eggs
3 c. coconut milk
1 tsp. vanilla
2 c. cooked and grated taro

Preheat oven to 350°. Grease a 9 x 13-inch pan. Melt butter and set aside. Combine mochiko, sugars and baking powder in a large mixing bowl. Add the margarine, coconut milk, vanilla, taro and eggs to flour mixture and mix well. Pour batter into prepared baking pan. Bake for 1 hour. Cool completely before cutting.

Tay doy

1 box mochiko
1¼ c. brown sugar
1½ c. hot water
½ c. sesame seeds
Fillings -
½ c. sweetened shredded coconut
½ c. roasted chopped peanuts
3 tsp. white sugar
oil for deep frying

Dissolve brown sugar in hot water. Cool. Put mochiko into a large mixing bowl. Pour enough liquid mixture into mochiko to make a stiff dough. Form dough into walnut size balls. Flatten balls. In a small mixing bowl, combine coconut, peanuts and 3 tsp. of white sugar. Place a teaspoon of filling on center of dough. Bring dough up and around filling. Pinch ends to seal. Roll balls in sesame seeds. Drop balls into heated oil and fry until golden brown. Drain and serve.

THAI SWEET RICE CUSTARD

1 c. mochi rice
1³/₄ c. coconut milk
1 tsp. salt
1 T. sugar
lime slice to garnish

Rinse mochi rice. Mix coconut milk with salt and sugar. Add mochi rice and stir. Steam rice mixture in rice cooker.

Custard

2 T. rose water
2 T. brown sugar
1³/₄ c. coconut milk
4 eggs, beaten

Preheat oven to 275°. Mix rose water and brown sugar with the coconut milk. Stir in eggs and beat well. Place custard in a casserole dish. Place casserole dish in a baking pan with about a ½ inch of water. Bake for about 1½ hours or until custard is set. To serve, put cooked custard on top of the rice and garnish with lime slices. This dish can be served hot or cold.

27324-99

Three chum cakes

6 T. mochiko
4 T. kinako
1 c. sweetened shredded coconut flakes
1/2 c. toasted sesame seeds
4 T. white sugar
3/4 c. mochiko
1/4 c. coconut milk
1 egg, beaten
1/4 tsp. salt
oil

Mix 6 T. mochiko, kinako and enough water to form a paste the consistency of heavy cream. Stir in the coconut flakes, sesame seeds and sugar. You may need to add more water in order to maintain a sticky consistency. Place pan over low heat, and continue to stir until the mixture becomes thick. The sugar will melt and a soft dough will form. Remove from heat. Cool mixture until you are able to handle. Roll dough into balls the size of large walnuts. Put aside. Place 3/4 c. mochiko and 1/4 c. coconut milk into a mixing bowl and stir. Beat in egg and salt. Dip mochi balls into this batter and deep fry until golden brown. Drain and serve warm.

THREE LAYERED MOCHI

3½ c. mochiko
2½ c. white sugar
1 tsp. baking powder
1 can coconut milk
2 c. water
2 tsp. vanilla
3 different food coloring dyes - any color

Preheat oven to 350°. In a large mixing bowl, mochiko, sugar and baking powder. Add coconut milk and water. Mix until well blended. Add vanilla. Mix. Divide batter into three parts. Put several drops of the first food coloring into the first bowl. Mix. Pour batter into a greased 9 x 13-inch pan. Cover pan with foil tightly. Bake for fifteen minutes. While the first layer is baking, add the second and third color choices to the last two bowls. Mix. Pour the second color layer over the first layer. Cover tightly with foil and bake for twenty minutes. Pour the third layer over the second layer. Cover tightly with foil and bake for thirty minutes. Remove from oven and cool before cutting.

TIKOY

32 oz. of mochiko
3 c. brown sugar
¼ tsp. salt
3 T. vanilla
5⅕ c. water
oil for frying

Combine mochiko, brown sugar and salt in a large mixing bowl. Add vanilla and half of the water. Begin to mix batter. Keep on adding water slowly to batter while mixing. Beat until mixture is smooth. Spray a round glass baking dish with cooking spray. Pour batter into glass dish. Place glass dish into a steamer pot and steam for one to two hours. Add water to pot as needed. Mochi will be done when it is firm to the touch. Let cool for at least two hours. Mochi will be soft. If you want it harder, leave it in the fridge for a day or two, then slice it it and fry it.

27324-99

TSUBUSHI-AN MOCHI

1 pkg. mochiko
3/4 c. white sugar
2 c. water
1 can Tsubushi-an
potato starch

Boil water and sugar together. Remove from heat and add mochiko. Stir until mixture is smooth. Cook an additional five to ten minutes on medium heat. Stir constantly. Pour mochi out onto a counter or cutting board that has been dusted with potato starch. Pinch off a piece of mochi and flatten out in hands that have been greased or coated with potato starch to prevent sticking. Place a teaspoonful of tsubushi-an on flattened mochi. Bring up sides and pinch together. Make sure mochi is well sealed. Place on a plate coated with potato starch, seam side down. Enjoy.

TSUBUSHIAN NANTU

4 c. mochiko
1 1/2 c. sugar
1 c. tsubushian
3 c. water
1/4 tsp. salt
kinako

Place mochiko, sugar and salt in a bowl. Add water gradually, kneading until a smooth dough forms. Add tsubushian and mix into dough. Place mixture on a wet cloth and steam for 30 minutes. Turn out onto a kinako covered counter. Sprinkle additional kinako on top. Cool before cutting.

Two layer nantu

8 c. mochiko
4 c. white sugar
1/4 tsp. salt
kinako
6 c. water
red food coloring

Mix together 4 c. mochiko, 2 c. sugar and 1/8 tsp. salt in one bowl. Gradually add 3 cups of water. Knead dough until it is smooth. Pour dough into a cheese cloth lined pan. Pan should be approximately 9 x 13-inch or a little smaller if your steamer is smaller. Steam for 20 minutes. In the mean time repeat the procedure for making the dough. This time add several drops of food coloring into dough and then knead. Mixture should be light pink in color. Place the second dough on top of first layer and steam an additional 40 minutes. Turn mochi out onto a kinako covered surface and cool before slicing. Add more kinako as desired.

Umukuji tempura

3 c. mochiko
3 c. mashed sweet potato
1 1/2 c. white sugar
1/4 tsp. salt
1/2 c. water
zest of 1 orange
oil

Wash and peel sweet potatoes. Soak in water with 1 tsp. of salt added. Drain and repeat this. Boil sweet potatoes, drain and mash potatoes. Add salt, sugar and mochiko to potatoes and mix. Combine zest and 1/2 c. water and gradually add to flour mixture. Mix well. Knead until dough is smooth and firm. Divide dough into 3 or 4 parts. Place dough on a dusted surface and flatten to a 1/2 inch in thickness. Cut into 2 1/2 inch lengths, slice in 1 inch widths. Deep fry in oil heated to 350°. Cool before eating.

27324-99

Umushi

3 c. mochiko
1 can koshi an
1½ c. flour
3 T. sugar
¼ tsp. salt
1½ c. water
ti leaves cut into 3 inch squares
oil

Brush ti leaves with oil and set aside. Mix mochiko, flour, sugar and salt in a mixing bowl. Add water and mix well. Knead dough for 3 minutes or until smooth. Shape dough into golf ball size balls. Dust hands and flatten balls. Place 1 tsp. bean paste in center and bring up edges. Pinch to seal. Place between 2 pieces of oiled ti leaf. Place on steamer rack and steam for 20 minutes.

Kazuko Adachi DeVirgilio

Umushi dango

3 c. mochiko
1½ c. flour
4 T. white sugar
1½ c. water
1 can Tsubushi-an
Pinch of salt
Several ti leaves or one banana leaf - washed out and cut into three squares oil

Oil leaves with oil and put aside. Mix mochiko, flour, sugar, and salt together. Add water and mix well. Knead dough for several minutes until smooth. Shape dough into balls - golf ball size. Dip hands into potato starch or cornstarch, flatten balls. Place one teaspoon of bean paste in center of dough. Pull up sides and pinch edges together to seal. Place dango between two oiled leaves. Place in steamer basket and steam for twenty minutes.

Yam Snowballs

20 oz. mochiko
2 c. white sugar
1 c. sweetened shredded coconut
6 eggs
4 pcs. canned yams drained
3 T. sesame seeds
oil for frying

Mix mochiko, sugar, coconut, eggs, yams, and sesame seeds together to form a dough. If dough is too stiff add a little of yam liquid. You should be able to make a patty out of dough. Form dough into patties and press sesame seeds into it. Fry until golden brown on both sides.

Yaman Gwashi

2 pkg. mochiko - 10 oz. each
1½ tsp. baking powder
3 c. grated mountain yam
2 eggs, beaten
3 c. sugar

Peel and grate yam. Add beaten eggs and sugar to yam and mix well. Add mochiko and baking powder. Mix thoroughly. Put in to 2 small grease loaf pans and place on a steamer rack in steamer. Steam for 30 minutes on high heat. Cool and serve.

27324-99

Yomogi mochi

1 bunch cleaned and steamed Yomogi leaves
1½ c. mochiko
¼ c. white sugar
1 tsp. baking soda
1½ c. water

In a medium saucepan bring approx. 2½ cups of water to boil. Add baking soda and Yomogi leaves. Cook until leaves are soft. Drain and chop leaves finely. Place leaves in a dish towel and ring out all additional moisture. In a mixing bowl combine mochiko, sugar and 1½ cups of water. Add yomogi leaves and mix well. Place mixture in a greased 8 x 8 glass or microwave pan. Microwave on HIGH for ten minutes. Cool. Cut with plastic knife and roll in potato starch.

Yomogi nantu

4 c. mochiko
1¾ c. white sugar
½ tsp. salt
3 c. water
½ c. yomogi leaves
kinako

Mix mochiko, water and salt until dough is smooth. Pour into a double layered cheesecloth and steam dough for 45 minutes. Immediately place steamed mochi into a mixing bowl and add sugar and mix well. Rinse and grind yomogi leaves in either blender or food processor. Add ground yomogi leaves to mochi mixture and mix. Pour mochi into a 9 x 13-inch pan that has been dusted with kinako. Sprinkle more kinako on top if desired. Let mochi set for at least 6 hours before cutting. Cut with a plastic knife.

Zenzai

1 c. cleaned Azuki beans
1½ c. white sugar
5 oz. mochiko
½ tsp. salt
Azuki beans -
1 c. Azuki beans
water

Cook Azuki beans in 2 quarts of hot water for about one hour. Remove from heat and cool. Add enough water to beans to make approximately 1½ quarts. Return beans to stove and cook until beans are tender. Add sugar and salt and bring to a boil. More water may be added if thinner consistency is desired. Mix mochiko with enough water to make a stiff dough. Knead dough. Form dough into small balls and drop into bean mixture. Cook until balls rise to the top of pot. Stir occasionally. Serve warm.

Recipe Favorites

27324-99

INDEX OF RECIPES

Mochi

HOW TO ORDER

Get your additional copies of this cookbook by returning an order form and your check or money order to:

Teresa DeVirgilio-Lam
5239 Kalanianaole Hwy.
Honolulu, HI 96821
THOR5239@AOL.COM (e-mail)

✂ -

Please send me _____ copies of the **Unbearably Good! Mochi Lovers Cookbook** at **$6.00** per copy and **$2.00** for shipping and handling per book. Enclosed is my check or money order for $_____.

Mail Books To:

Name _____

Address _____

City _____ State _____ Zip _____

✂ -

Please send me _____ copies of the **Unbearably Good! Mochi Lovers Cookbook** at **$6.00** per copy and **$2.00** for shipping and handling per book. Enclosed is my check or money order for $_____.

Mail Books To:

Name _____

Address _____

City _____ State _____ Zip _____

27324 j

Cooking Tips

1. After stewing a chicken, cool in broth before cutting into chunks; it will have twice the flavor.

2. To slice meat into thin strips, as for stir-fry dishes, partially freeze it so it will slice more easily.

3. A roast with the bone in will cook faster than a boneless roast. The bone carries the heat to the inside more quickly.

4. Never cook a cold roast. Let it stand for at least an hour at room temperature. Brush with oil before and during roasting; the oil will seal in the juices.

5. For a juicier hamburger, add cold water to the beef before grilling (½ cup to 1 pound of meat).

6. To freeze meatballs, place them on a cookie sheet until frozen. Place in plastic bags. They will stay separated so that you may remove as many as you want.

7. To keep cauliflower white while cooking, add a little milk to the water.

8. When boiling corn, add sugar to the water instead of salt. Salt will toughen the corn.

9. To ripen tomatoes, put them in a brown paper bag in a dark pantry, and they will ripen overnight.

10. To keep celery crisp, stand it upright in a pitcher of cold, salted water and refrigerate.

11. When cooking cabbage, place a small tin cup or can half full of vinegar on the stove near the cabbage. It will absorb the odor.

12. Potatoes soaked in salt water for 20 minutes before baking will bake more rapidly.

13. Let raw potatoes stand in cold water for at least a half-hour before frying in order to improve the crispness of French-fried potatoes. Dry potatoes thoroughly before adding to oil.

14. Use greased muffin tins as molds when baking stuffed green peppers.

15. A few drops of lemon juice in the water will whiten boiled potatoes.

16. Buy mushrooms before they "open." When stems and caps are attached firmly, mushrooms are truly fresh.

17. Do not use metal bowls when mixing salads. Use wood, glass or china.

18. Lettuce keeps better if you store it in the refrigerator without washing it. Keep the leaves dry. Wash lettuce the day you are going to use it.

19. Do not use soda to keep vegetables green. It destroys Vitamin C.

20. Do not despair if you oversalt gravy. Stir in some instant mashed potatoes to repair the damage. Just add a little more liquid in order to offset the thickening.

Herbs & Spices

Acquaint yourself with herbs and spices. Add in small amounts, 1/4 teaspoon for every 4 servings. Crush dried herbs or snip fresh ones before using. Use 3 times more fresh herbs if substituting fresh for dried.

Basil Sweet, warm flavor with an aromatic odor. Use whole or ground. Good with lamb, fish, roast, stews, ground beef, vegetables, dressing and omelets.

Bay Leaves Pungent flavor. Use whole leaf but remove before serving. Good in vegetable dishes, seafood, stews and pickles.

Caraway Spicy taste and aromatic smell. Use in cakes, breads, soups, cheese and sauerkraut.

Chives Sweet, mild flavor like that of onion. Excellent in salads, fish, soups and potatoes.

Cilantro Use fresh. Excellent in salads, fish, chicken, rice, beans and Mexican dishes.

Curry Powder Spices are combined to proper proportions to give a distinct flavor to meat, poultry, fish and vegetables.

Dill Both seeds and leaves are flavorful. Leaves may be used as a garnish or cooked with fish, soup, dressings, potatoes and beans. Leaves or the whole plant may be used to flavor pickles.

Fennel Sweet, hot flavor. Both seeds and leaves are used. Use in small quantities in pies and baked goods. Leaves can be boiled with fish.

Ginger A pungent root, this aromatic spice is sold fresh, dried or ground. Use in pickles, preserves, cakes, cookies, soups and meat dishes.

Herbs & Spices

Marjoram   May be used both dried or green. Use to flavor fish, poultry, omelets, lamb, stew, stuffing and tomato juice.

Mint   Aromatic with a cool flavor. Excellent in beverages, fish, lamb, cheese, soup, peas, carrots, and fruit desserts.

Oregano   Strong, aromatic odor. Use whole or ground in tomato juice, fish, eggs, pizza, omelets, chili, stew, gravy, poultry and vegetables.

Paprika   A bright red pepper, this spice is used in meat, vegetables and soups or as a garnish for potatoes, salads or eggs.

Parsley   Best when used fresh, but can be used dried as a garnish or as a seasoning. Try in fish, omelets, soup, meat, stuffing and mixed greens.

Rosemary   Very aromatic. Can be used fresh or dried. Season fish, stuffing, beef, lamb, poultry, onions, eggs, bread and potatoes. Great in dressings.

Saffron   Orange-yellow in color, this spice flavors or colors foods. Use in soup, chicken, rice and breads.

Sage   Use fresh or dried. The flowers are sometimes used in salads. May be used in tomato juice, fish, omelets, beef, poultry, stuffing, cheese spreads and breads.

Tarragon   Leaves have a pungent, hot taste. Use to flavor sauces, salads, fish, poultry, tomatoes, eggs, green beans, carrots and dressings.

Thyme   Sprinkle leaves on fish or poultry before broiling or baking. Throw a few sprigs directly on coals shortly before meat is finished grilling.

Baking Breads

Hints for Baking Breads

1. Kneading dough for 30 seconds after mixing improves the texture of baking powder biscuits.

2. Instead of shortening, use cooking or salad oil in waffles and hot cakes.

3. When bread is baking, a small dish of water in the oven will help keep the crust from hardening.

4. Dip a spoon in hot water to measure shortening, butter, etc., and the fat will slip out more easily.

5. Small amounts of leftover corn may be added to pancake batter for variety.

6. To make bread crumbs, use the fine cutter of a food grinder and tie a large paper bag over the spout in order to prevent flying crumbs.

7. When you are doing any sort of baking, you get better results if you remember to preheat your cookie sheet, muffin tins or cake pans.

Rules for Use of Leavening Agents

1. In simple flour mixtures, use 2 teaspoons baking powder to leaven 1 cup flour. Reduce this amount 1/2 teaspoon for each egg used.

2. To 1 teaspoon soda use 2 1/4 teaspoons cream of tartar, 2 cups freshly soured milk, or 1 cup molasses.

3. To substitute soda and an acid for baking powder, divide the amount of baking powder by 4. Take that as your measure and add acid according to rule 2.

Proportions of Baking Powder to Flour

biscuits ....to 1 cup flour use 1 1/4 tsp. baking powder
cake with oil ....to 1 cup flour use 1 tsp. baking powder
muffins ....to 1 cup flour use 1 1/2 tsp. baking powder
popovers ....to 1 cup flour use 1 1/4 tsp. baking powder
waffles ....to 1 cup flour use 1 1/4 tsp. baking powder

Proportions of Liquid to Flour

drop batter ....to 1 cup liquid use 2 to 2 1/2 cups flour
pour batter ....to 1 cup liquid use 1 cup flour
soft dough ....to 1 cup liquid use 3 to 3 1/2 cups flour
stiff dough ....to 1 cup liquid use 4 cups flour

Time and Temperature Chart

Breads	Minutes	Temperature
biscuits	12 - 15	400° - 450°
cornbread	25 - 30	400° - 425°
gingerbread	40 - 50	350° - 370°
loaf	50 - 60	350° - 400°
nut bread	50 - 75	350°
popovers	30 - 40	425° - 450°
rolls	20 - 30	400° - 450°

Baking Desserts

Perfect Cookies

Cookie dough that is to be rolled is much easier to handle after it has been refrigerated for 10 to 30 minutes. This keeps the dough from sticking, even though it may be soft. If not done, the soft dough may require more flour and too much flour makes cookies hard and brittle. Place on a floured board only as much dough as can be easily managed. Flour the rolling pin slightly and roll lightly to desired thickness. Cut shapes close together and add trimmings to dough that needs to be rolled. Place pans or sheets in upper third of oven. Watch cookies carefully while baking in order to avoid burned edges. When sprinkling sugar on cookies, try putting it into a salt shaker in order to save time.

Perfect Pies

1. Pie crust will be better and easier to make if all the ingredients are cool.

2. The lower crust should be placed in the pan so that it covers the surface smoothly. Air pockets beneath the surface will push the crust out of shape while baking.

3. Folding the top crust over the lower crust before crimping will keep juices in the pie.

4. In making custard pie, bake at a high temperature for about ten minutes to prevent a soggy crust. Then finish baking at a low temperature.

5. When making cream pie, sprinkle crust with powdered sugar in order to prevent it from becoming soggy.

Perfect Cakes

1. Fill cake pans two-thirds full and spread batter into corners and sides, leaving a slight hollow in the center.

2. Cake is done when it shrinks from the sides of the pan or if it springs back when touched lightly with the finger.

3. After removing a cake from the oven, place it on a rack for about five minutes. Then, the sides should be loosened and the cake turned out on a rack in order to finish cooling.

4. Do not frost cakes until thoroughly cool.

5. Icing will remain where you put it if you sprinkle cake with powdered sugar first.

Time and Temperature Chart

Dessert	Time	Temperature
butter cake, layer	20-40 min.	380° - 400°
butter cake, loaf	40-60 min.	360° - 400°
cake, angel	50-60 min.	300° - 360°
cake, fruit	3-4 hrs.	275° - 325°
cake, sponge	40-60 min.	300° - 350°
cookies, molasses	18-20 min.	350° - 375°
cookies, thin	10-12 min.	380° - 390°
cream puffs	45-60 min.	300° - 350°
meringue	40-60 min.	250° - 300°
pie crust	20-40 min.	400° - 500°

Vegetables & Fruits

Vegetable	Cooking Method	Time
artichokes	boiled	40 min.
	steamed	45-60 min.
asparagus tips	boiled	10-15 min.
beans, lima	boiled	20-40 min.
	steamed	60 min.
beans, string	boiled	15-35 min.
	steamed	60 min.
beets, old	boiled or steamed	1-2 hours
beets, young with skin	boiled	30 min.
	steamed	60 min.
	baked	70-90 min.
broccoli, flowerets	boiled	5-10 min.
broccoli, stems	boiled	20-30 min.
brussels sprouts	boiled	20-30 min.
cabbage, chopped	boiled	10-20 min.
	steamed	25 min.
carrots, cut across	boiled	8-10 min.
	steamed	40 min.
cauliflower, flowerets	boiled	8-10 min.
cauliflower, stem down	boiled	20-30 min.
corn, green, tender	boiled	5-10 min.
	steamed	15 min.
	baked	20 min.
corn on the cob	boiled	8-10 min.
	steamed	15 min.
eggplant, whole	boiled	30 min.
	steamed	40 min.
	baked	45 min.
parsnips	boiled	25-40 min.
	steamed	60 min.
	baked	60-75 min.
peas, green	boiled or steamed	5-15 min.
potatoes	boiled	20-40 min.
	steamed	60 min.
	baked	45-60 min.
pumpkin or squash	boiled	20-40 min.
	steamed	45 min.
	baked	60 min.
tomatoes	boiled	5-15 min.
turnips	boiled	25-40 min.

Drying Time Table

Fruit	Sugar or Honey	Cooking Time
apricots	¼ c. for each cup of fruit	about 40 min.
figs	1 T. for each cup of fruit	about 30 min.
peaches	¼ c. for each cup of fruit	about 45 min.
prunes	2 T. for each cup of fruit	about 45 min.

Vegetables & Fruits

Buying Fresh Vegetables

Artichokes: Look for compact, tightly closed heads with green, clean-looking leaves. Avoid those with leaves that are brown or separated.

Asparagus: Stalks should be tender and firm; tips should be close and compact. Choose the stalks with very little white; they are more tender. Use asparagus soon because it toughens rapidly.

Beans, Snap: Those with small seeds inside the pods are best. Avoid beans with dry-looking pods.

Broccoli, Brussels Sprouts and Cauliflower: Flower clusters on broccoli and cauliflower should be tight and close together. Brussels sprouts should be firm and compact. Smudgy, dirty spots may indicate pests or disease.

Cabbage and Head Lettuce: Choose heads that are heavy for their size. Avoid cabbage with worm holes and lettuce with discoloration or soft rot.

Cucumbers: Choose long, slender cucumbers for best quality. May be dark or medium green, but yellow ones are undesirable.

Mushrooms: Caps should be closed around the stems. Avoid black or brown gills.

Peas and Lima Beans: Select pods that are well-filled but not bulging. Avoid dried, spotted, yellow, or flabby pods.

Buying Fresh Fruits

Bananas: Skin should be free of bruises and black or brown spots. Purchase them green and allow them to ripen at home at room temperature.

Berries: Select plump, solid berries with good color. Avoid stained containers which indicate wet or leaky berries. Berries with clinging caps, such as blackberries and raspberries, may be unripe. Strawberries without caps may be overripe.

Melons: In cantaloupes, thick, close netting on the rind indicates best quality. Cantaloupes are ripe when the stem scar is smooth and the space between the netting is yellow or yellow-green. They are best when fully ripe with fruity odor.

Honeydews are ripe when rind has creamy to yellowish color and velvety texture. Immature honeydews are whitish-green.

Ripe watermelons have some yellow color on one side. If melons are white or pale green on one side, they are not ripe.

Oranges, Grapefruit and Lemons: Choose those heavy for their size. Smoother, thinner skins usually indicate more juice. Most skin markings do not affect quality. Oranges with a slight greenish tinge may be just as ripe as fully colored ones. Light or greenish-yellow lemons are more tart than deep yellow ones. Avoid citrus fruits showing withered, sunken or soft areas.

Napkin Folding

General Tips:
Use well-starched linen napkins if possible. For more complicated folds, 24-inch napkins work best. Practice the folds with newspapers. Children can help. Once they learn the folds, they will have fun!

Shield

Easy fold. Elegant with monogram in corner.

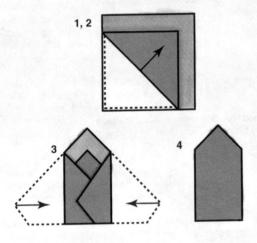

Instructions:
1. Fold into quarter size. If monogrammed, ornate corner should face down.
2. Turn up folded corner three-quarters.
3. Overlap right side and left side points.
4. Turn over; adjust sides so that they are even, single point in center.
5. Place point up or down on plate, or left of plate.

Rosette

Elegant on plate.

Instructions:
1. Fold left and right edges to center, leaving ½" opening along center.
2. Pleat firmly from top edge to bottom edge. Sharpen edges with hot iron.
3. Pinch center together. If necessary, use small piece of pipe cleaner to secure and top with single flower.
4. Spread out rosette.

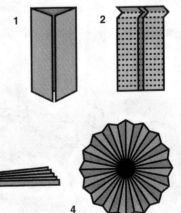

Napkin Folding

Candle

Easy to do; can be decorated.

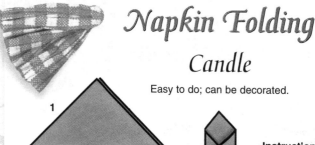

Instructions:
1. Fold into triangle, point at top.
2. Turn lower edge up 1".
3. Turn over, folded edge down.
4. Roll tightly from left to right.
5. Tuck in corner. Stand upright.

Fan

Pretty in napkin ring or on plate.

Instructions:
1. Fold top and bottom edges to center.
2. Fold top and bottom edges to center a second time.
3. Pleat firmly from the left edge. Sharpen edges with hot iron.
4. Spread out fan. Balance flat folds of each side on table. Well-starched napkins will hold shape.

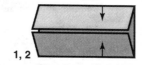

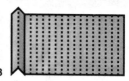

Lily

Effective and pretty on table.

Instructions:
1. Fold napkin into quarters.
2. Fold into triangle, closed corner to open points.
3. Turn two points over to other side. (Two points are on either side of closed point.)
4. Pleat.
5. Place closed end in glass. Pull down two points on each side and shape.

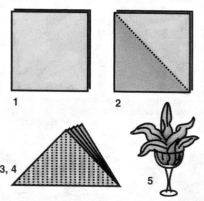

Measurements & Substitutions

Measurements

a pinch	⅛ teaspoon or less
3 teaspoons	1 tablespoon
4 tablespoons	¼ cup
8 tablespoons	½ cup
12 tablespoons	¾ cup
16 tablespoons	1 cup
2 cups	1 pint
4 cups	1 quart
4 quarts	1 gallon
8 quarts	1 peck
4 pecks	1 bushel
16 ounces	1 pound
32 ounces	1 quart
1 ounce liquid	2 tablespoons
8 ounces liquid	1 cup

**Use standard measuring spoons and cups.
All measurements are level.**

Substitutions

Ingredient	Quantity	Substitute
baking powder	1 teaspoon	¼ tsp. baking soda plus ½ tsp. cream of tartar
catsup or chili sauce	1 cup	1 c. tomato sauce plus ½ c. sugar and 2 T. vinegar (for use in cooking)
chocolate	1 square (1 oz.)	3 or 4 T. cocoa plus 1 T. butter
cornstarch	1 tablespoon	2 T. flour or 2 tsp. quick-cooking tapioca
cracker crumbs	¾ cup	1 c. bread crumbs
dates	1 lb.	1 ½ c. dates, pitted and cut
dry mustard	1 teaspoon	1 T. prepared mustard
flour, self-rising	1 cup	1 c. all-purpose flour, ½ tsp. salt, and 1 tsp. baking powder
herbs, fresh	1 tablespoon	1 tsp. dried herbs
milk, sour	1 cup	1 T. lemon juice or vinegar plus sweet milk to make 1 c. (let stand 5 minutes)
whole	1 cup	½ c. evaporated milk plus ½ c. water
min. marshmallows	10	1 lg. marshmallow
onion, fresh	1 small	1 T. instant minced onion, rehydrated
sugar, brown	½ cup	2 T. molasses in ½ c. granulated sugar
powdered	1 cup	1 c. granulated sugar plus 1 tsp. cornstarch
tomato juice	1 cup	½ c. tomato sauce plus ½ c. water

**When substituting cocoa for chocolate in cakes, the amount of flour must
be reduced. Brown and white sugars usually can be interchanged.**

Equivalency Chart

Food	Quantity	Yield
apple	1 medium	1 cup
banana, mashed	1 medium	1/3 cup
bread	1 1/2 slices	1 cup soft crumbs
bread	1 slice	1/4 cup fine, dry crumbs
butter	1 stick or 1/4 pound	1/2 cup
cheese, American, cubed	1 pound	2 2/3 cups
American, grated	1 pound	5 cups
cream cheese	3-ounce package	6 2/3 tablespoons
chocolate, bitter	1 square	1 ounce
cocoa	1 pound	4 cups
coconut	1 1/2 pound package	2 2/3 cups
coffee, ground	1 pound	5 cups
cornmeal	1 pound	3 cups
cornstarch	1 pound	3 cups
crackers, graham	14 squares	1 cup fine crumbs
saltine	28 crackers	1 cup fine crumbs
egg	4-5 whole	1 cup
whites	8-10	1 cup
yolks	10-12	1 cup
evaporated milk	1 cup	3 cups whipped
flour, cake, sifted	1 pound	4 1/2 cups
rye	1 pound	5 cups
white, sifted	1 pound	4 cups
white, unsifted	1 pound	3 3/4 cups
gelatin, flavored	3 1/4 ounces	1/2 cup
unflavored	1/4 ounce	1 tablespoon
lemon	1 medium	3 tablespoon juice
marshmallows	16	1/4 pound
noodles, cooked	8-ounce package	7 cups
uncooked	4 ounces (1 1/2 cups)	2-3 cups cooked
macaroni, cooked	8-ounce package	6 cups
macaroni, uncooked	4 ounces (1 1/4 cups)	2 1/4 cups cooked
spaghetti, uncooked	7 ounces	4 cups cooked
nuts, chopped	1/4 pound	1 cup
almonds	1 pound	3 1/2 cups
walnuts, broken	1 pound	3 cups
walnuts, unshelled	1 pound	1 1/2 to 1 3/4 cups
onion	1 medium	1/2 cup
orange	3-4 medium	1 cup juice
raisins	1 pound	3 1/2 cups
rice, brown	1 cup	4 cups cooked
converted	1 cup	3 1/2 cups cooked
regular	1 cup	3 cups cooked
wild	1 cup	4 cups cooked
sugar, brown	1 pound	2 1/2 cups
powdered	1 pound	3 1/2 cups
white	1 pound	2 cups
vanilla wafers	22	1 cup fine crumbs
zwieback, crumbled	4	1 cups

Food Quantities
For Large Servings

	25 Servings	50 Servings	100 Servings
Beverages:			
coffee	½ pound and 1 ½ gallons water	1 pound and 3 gallons water	2 pounds and 6 gallons water
lemonade	10-15 lemons and 1 ½ gallons water	20-30 lemons and 3 gallons water	40-60 lemons and 6 gallons water
tea	1/12 pound and 1 ½ gallons water	1/6 pound and 3 gallons water	1/3 pound and 6 gallons water
Desserts:			
layered cake	1 12" cake	3 10" cakes	6 10" cakes
sheet cake	1 10" x 12" cake	1 12" x 20" cake	2 12" x 20" cakes
watermelon	37 ½ pounds	75 pounds	150 pounds
whipping cream	¾ pint	1 ½ to 2 pints	3-4 pints
Ice cream:			
brick	3 ¼ quarts	6 ½ quarts	13 quarts
bulk	2 ¼ quarts	4 ½ quarts or 1 ¼ gallons	9 quarts or 2 ½ gallons
Meat, poultry or fish:			
fish	13 pounds	25 pounds	50 pounds
fish, fillets or steak	7 ½ pounds	15 pounds	30 pounds
hamburger	9 pounds	18 pounds	35 pounds
turkey or chicken	13 pounds	25 to 35 pounds	50 to 75 pounds
wieners (beef)	6 ½ pounds	13 pounds	25 pounds
Salads, casseroles:			
baked beans	¾ gallon	1 ¼ gallons	2 ½ gallons
jello salad	¾ gallon	1 ¼ gallons	2 ½ gallons
potato salad	4 ¼ quarts	2 ¼ gallons	4 ½ gallons
scalloped potatoes	4 ½ quarts or 1 12" x 20" pan	9 quarts or 2 ¼ gallons	18 quarts 4 ½ gallons
spaghetti	1 ¼ gallons	2 ½ gallons	5 gallons
Sandwiches:			
bread	50 slices or 3 1-pound loaves	100 slices or 6 1-pound loaves	200 slices or 12 1-pound loaves
butter	½ pound	1 pound	2 pounds
lettuce	1 ½ heads	3 heads	6 heads
mayonnaise	1 cup	2 cups	4 cups
mixed filling			
meat, eggs, fish	1 ½ quarts	3 quarts	6 quarts
jam, jelly	1 quart	2 quarts	4 quarts

Microwave Hints

1. Place an open box of hardened brown sugar in the microwave oven with 1 cup hot water. Microwave on high for 1 1/2 to 2 minutes for 1/2 pound or 2 to 3 minutes for 1 pound.

2. Soften hard ice cream by microwaving at 30% power. One pint will take 15 to 30 seconds; one quart, 30-45 seconds; and one-half gallon, 45-60 seconds.

3. To melt chocolate, place 1/2 pound in glass bowl or measuring cup. Melt uncovered at 50% power for 3-4 minutes; stir after 2 minutes.

4. Soften one 8-ounce package of cream cheese by microwaving at 30% power for 2 to 2 1/2 minutes. One 3-ounce package of cream cheese will soften in 1 1/2 to 2 minutes.

5. A 4 1/2 ounce carton of whipped topping will thaw in 1 minute on the defrost setting. Whipped topping should be slightly firm in the center, but it will blend well when stirred. Do not over thaw!

6. Soften jello that has set up too hard - perhaps you were to chill it until slightly thickened and forgot it. Heat on a low power setting for a very short time.

7. Heat hot packs. A wet fingertip towel will take about 25 seconds. It depends on the temperature of the water used to wet the towel.

8. To scald milk, cook 1 cup for 2 to 2 1/2 minutes, stirring once each minute.

9. To make dry bread crumbs, cut 6 slices of bread into 1/2-inch cubes. Microwave in 3-quart casserole 6-7 minutes, or until dry, stirring after 3 minutes. Crush in blender.

10. Refresh stale potato chips, crackers or other snacks of such type by putting a plateful in the microwave for 30-45 seconds. Let stand for 1 minute to crisp. Cereals can also be crisped.

11. Nuts will be easier to shell if you place 2 cups of nuts in a 1-quart casserole with 1 cup of water. Cook for 4 to 5 minutes and the nutmeats will slip out whole after cracking the shell.

12. Stamp collectors can place a few drops of water on a stamp to remove it from an envelope. Heat in the microwave for 20 seconds, and the stamp will come off.

13. Using a round dish instead of a square one eliminates overcooked corners in baking cakes.

14. Sprinkle a layer of medium, finely chopped walnuts evenly onto the bottom and side of a ring pan or bundt cake pan to enhances the looks and eating quality. Pour in batter and microwave as recipe directs.

15. Do not salt foods on the surface as it causes dehydration and toughens food. Salt after you remove from the oven unless the recipe calls for using salt in the mixture.

16. Heat left-over custard and use it as frosting for a cake.

17. Melt marshmallow cream. Half of a 7-ounce jar will melt in 35-40 seconds on high. Stir to blend.

18. To toast coconut, spread 1/2 cup coconut in a pie plate and cook for 3-4 minutes, stirring every 30 seconds after 2 minutes. Watch closely, as it quickly browns.

19. To melt crystallized honey, heat uncovered jar on high for 30-45 seconds. If jar is large, repeat.

20. One stick of butter or margarine will soften in 1 minute when microwaved at 20% power.

Calorie Counter

Beverages

apple juice, 6 oz.	90
coffee (black)	0
cola type, 12 oz.	115
cranberry juice, 6 oz.	115
ginger ale, 12 oz.	115
grape juice, (prepared from frozen concentrate), 6 oz.	142
lemonade, (prepared from frozen concentrate), 6 oz.	85
milk, protein fortified, 1 c.	105
skim, 1 c.	90
whole, 1 c.	160
orange juice, 6 oz.	85
pineapple juice, unsweetened, 6 oz.	95
root beer, 12 oz.	150
tonic (quinine water) 12 oz.	132

Breads

cornbread, 1 sm. square	130
dumplings, 1 med.	70
French toast, 1 slice	135
melba toast, 1 slice	25
muffins, blueberry, 1 muffin	110
bran, 1 muffin	106
corn, 1 muffin	125
English, 1 muffin	280
pancakes, 1 (4-in.)	60
pumpernickel, 1 slice	75
rye, 1 slice	60
waffle, 1	216
white, 1 slice	60-70
whole wheat, 1 slice	55-65

Cereals

cornflakes, 1 c.	105
cream of wheat, 1 c.	120
oatmeal, 1 c.	148
rice flakes, 1 c.	105
shredded wheat, 1 biscuit	100
sugar krisps, 3/4 c.	110

Crackers

graham, 1 cracker	15-30
rye crisp, 1 cracker	35
saltine, 1 cracker	17-20
wheat thins, 1 cracker	9

Dairy Products

butter or margarine, 1 T.	100
cheese, American, 1 oz.	100
camembert, 1 oz.	85
cheddar, 1 oz.	115
cottage cheese, 1 oz.	30
mozzarella, 1 oz.	90
parmesan, 1 oz.	130
ricotta, 1 oz.	50
roquefort, 1 oz.	105
Swiss, 1 oz.	105
cream, light, 1 T.	30
heavy, 1 T.	55
sour, 1 T.	45
hot chocolate, with milk, 1 c.	277
milk chocolate, 1 oz.	145-155
yogurt	
made w/ whole milk, 1 c.	150-165
made w/ skimmed milk, 1 c.	125

Eggs

fried, 1 lg.	100
poached or boiled, 1 lg.	75-80
scrambled or in omelet, 1 lg.	110-130

Fish and Seafood

bass, 4 oz.	105
salmon, broiled or baked, 3 oz.	155
sardines, canned in oil, 3 oz.	170
trout, fried, 3 1/2 oz.	220
tuna, in oil, 3 oz.	170
in water, 3 oz.	110

Calorie Counter

Fruits

apple, 1 med. 80-100
applesauce, sweetened, ½ c. 90-115
    unsweetened, ½ c..........................50
banana, 1 med. 85
blueberries, ½ c..............................45
cantaloupe, ½ c..............................24
cherries (pitted), raw, ½ c. 40
grapefruit, ½ med. 55
grapes, ½ c.................................35-55
honeydew, ½ c.................................55
mango, 1 med. 90
orange, 1 med. 65-75
peach, 1 med. 35
pear, 1 med. 60-100
pineapple, fresh, ½ c..........................40
    canned in syrup, ½ c. 95
plum, 1 med. 30
strawberries, fresh, ½ c.......................30
    frozen and sweetened, ½ c. 120-140
tangerine, 1 lg. 39
watermelon, ½ c. 42

Meat and Poultry

beef, ground (lean), 3 oz. 185
    roast, 3 oz. 185
chicken, broiled, 3 oz. 115
lamb chop (lean), 3 oz. 175-200
steak, sirloin, 3 oz. 175
    tenderloin, 3 oz. 174
    top round, 3 oz. 162
turkey, dark meat, 3 oz. 175
    white meat, 3 oz. 150
veal, cutlet, 3 oz..............................156
    roast, 3 oz. 76

Nuts

almonds, 2 T. 105
cashews, 2 T. 100
peanuts, 2 T. 105
peanut butter, 1 T...............................95
pecans, 2 T. 95
pistachios, 2 T. 92
walnuts, 2 T. 80

Pasta

macaroni or spaghetti,
    cooked, ¾ c. 115

Salad Dressings

blue cheese, 1 T. 70
French, 1 T......................................65
Italian, 1 T. 80
mayonnaise, 1 T. 100
olive oil, 1 T...................................124
Russian, 1 T.....................................70
salad oil, 1 T...................................120

Soups

bean, 1 c. 130-180
beef noodle, 1 c................................70
bouillon and consomme, 1 c. 30
chicken noodle, 1 c. 65
chicken with rice, 1 c. 50
minestrone, 1 c...........................80-150
split pea, 1 c............................145-170
tomato with milk, 1 c. 170
vegetable, 1 c. 80-100

Vegetables

asparagus, 1 c..................................35
broccoli, cooked, ½ c. 25
cabbage, cooked, ½ c. 15-20
carrots, cooked, ½ c. 25-30
cauliflower, ½ c. 10-15
corn (kernels), ½ c. 70
green beans, 1 c. 30
lettuce, shredded, ½ c..........................5
mushrooms, canned, ½ c. 20
onions, cooked, ½ c. 30
peas, cooked, ½ c...............................60
potato, baked, 1 med. 90
    chips, 8-10 100
    mashed, w/milk & butter, 1 c. ..200-300
spinach, 1 c....................................40
tomato, raw, 1 med. 25
    cooked, ½ c. 30

Cooking Terms

Au gratin: Topped with crumbs and/or cheese and browned in oven or under broiler.

Au jus: Served in its own juices.

Baste: To moisten foods during cooking with pan drippings or special sauce in order to add flavor and prevent drying.

Bisque: A thick cream soup.

Blanch: To immerse in rapidly boiling water and allow to cook slightly.

Cream: To soften a fat, especially butter, by beating it at room temperature. Butter and sugar are often creamed together, making a smooth, soft paste.

Crimp: To seal the edges of a two-crust pie either by pinching them at intervals with the fingers or by pressing them together with the tines of a fork.

Crudites: An assortment of raw vegetables (i.e. carrots, broccoli, celery, mushrooms) that is served as an hors d'oeuvre, often accompanied by a dip.

Degrease: To remove fat from the surface of stews, soups, or stock. Usually cooled in the refrigerator so that fat hardens and is easily removed.

Dredge: To coat lightly with flour, cornmeal, etc.

Entree: The main course.

Fold: To incorporate a delicate substance, such as whipped cream or beaten egg whites, into another substance without releasing air bubbles. A spatula is used to gently bring part of the mixture from the bottom of the bowl to the top. The process is repeated, while slowly rotating the bowl, until the ingredients are thoroughly blended.

Glaze: To cover with a glossy coating, such as a melted and somewhat diluted jelly for fruit desserts.

Julienne: To cut vegetables, fruits, or cheeses into match-shaped slivers.

Marinate: To allow food to stand in a liquid in order to tenderize or to add flavor.

Meuniére: Dredged with flour and sautéed in butter.

Mince: To chop food into very small pieces.

Parboil: To boil until partially cooked; to blanch. Usually final cooking in a seasoned sauce follows this procedure.

Pare: To remove the outermost skin of a fruit or vegetable.

Poach: To cook gently in hot liquid kept just below the boiling point.

Purée: To mash foods by hand by rubbing through a sieve or food mill, or by whirling in a blender or food processor until perfectly smooth.

Refresh: To run cold water over food that has been parboiled in order to stop the cooking process quickly.

Sauté: To cook and/or brown food in a small quantity of hot shortening.

Scald: To heat to just below the boiling point, when tiny bubbles appear at the edge of the saucepan.

Simmer: To cook in liquid just below the boiling point. The surface of the liquid should be barely moving, broken from time to time by slowly rising bubbles.

Steep: To let food stand in hot liquid in order to extract or to enhance flavor, like tea in hot water or poached fruit in sugar syrup.

Toss: To combine ingredients with a repeated lifting motion.

Whip: To beat rapidly in order to incorporate air and produce expansion, as in heavy cream or egg whites.